UNRECOGNIZED RESISTANCE

UNRECOGNIZED RESISTANCE

The Franco-American Experience in World War Two

Edited and with an introduction by
François-Georges Dreyfus

Translated by Paul Seaton

Transaction Publishers
New Brunswick (U.S.A.) and London (U.K.)

Library of Congress Catalog Number: 2004047868
ISBN: 0-7658-0240-6
Printed in the United States of America

Library of Congress Cataloging-in-Publication Data

Colloque sur la "nébuleuse du dévouement" (2000) : Paris, France)
    [Colloque sur la "nébuleuse du dévouement." English]
      Unrecognized resistance : the Franco-American experience in World War Two / edited and with an introduction by François-Georges Dreyfus ; translated by Paul Seaton.
      p. cm.
      Proceedings of the Colloque sur la "nébuleuse du dévouement" sponsored by the Club Témoin and the Hoover Institution on Dec. 4, 2000, in Paris.
      ISBN 0-7658-0240-6 (alk. paper)
      1. World War, 1939-1945—Underground movements—France—Congresses. 2. World War, 1939-1945—Personal narratives, French—Congresses. I. Dreyfus, François G. II. Club Témoin. III. Hoover Institution on War, Revolution, and Peace. IV. Title.

D802.F8C584   2000
940.53'44—dc22   2004047868

We would especially like to thank the following for their assistance in organizing the colloquium:

The Hoover Institution,
Christian Poncelet, president of the French Senate,
the services of the Senate,
the donors of the Club Témoin,
the Avenance Society,
the Maury-Imprimeur Society,
the Air France Group,
and Patrice de Plunkett, moderator of the colloquium.

Contents

Translator's Note

I would not be the first translator who has to make the awkward confession that his efforts encountered from the first step an unavoidable snare.[1] The title of the following collection in French is *La nébuleuse du dévouement*. I have chosen to translate it as *Unrecognized Resistance*, which adequately conveys its meaning to the American reader. The English phrase, however, loses important aspects—and charms—of the French original.

As many contributors note, it is a (quintessentially French) phrase from Mr. Jacques Debû-Bridel, writer, journalist, and leader in the French Resistance.[2] In a famous phrase, he refers to the *civilian* Resistance, to the moral and material support given him and his fellow underground resisters by innumerable members of the general population, as "a current of sympathy, a nebula of sympathy, a nebula of devotion" without which he and they would not have been able to survive and operate. Others, though, extend and complicate the meaning of the phrase. To indicate reasons for this, a bit of etymology is useful.

The first term, "nébuleuse," is an adjective become a noun. It comes from a Latin word meaning "fog" or "mist," that is, a ground hugging and covering "cloud" (another meaning of the term); our English word, "nebulous," meaning vague, obviously shares that root. From there it was ascribed to certain celestial phenomena that we designate by the Latinate English term "nebula/ae." Various contributors take the word sometimes in its root denotation, sometimes in its derivative meanings. That is, some emphasize the obscure, therefore sheltering, mists of French resistance; others like to highlight its organized aspects in "chains," "circuits," and "networks." Some intend "fog," others write "constellation."

The second term of the phrase also has an obvious English cousin, "devotion," and the French cluster of meanings remains squarely in that semantic territory: "loyalty," "devotion," "sacrifice."

ix

The combined phrase and concept thus is rather complicated. It connotes more than one set of meanings, which need to be distinguished, then combined and kept in mind by the American reader. On the one hand, the full designation refers to the deliberately obscure resisters, organized and not, militant and not, underground or not, who kept alive French honor internally during the war by various acts of "opposition," both to the Vichy government and to the German occupiers. As such, they were (and were intended to be) invisible to those they struggled against. They operated in, and as, a mist or fog of opposition.

That opposition, though, frequently took the form of, and always drew from, loyalty and devotion to others and to France. It entailed the risk and often exacted the full price of sacrifice. Thus, on the other hand, they were a "public presence" to the wider French populace. Frequently known by the general population, they provided much needed moral tone and support to their beleaguered countrymen. And in turn they received "aid and comfort" from the latter in manifold ways. These nebulae/mists were mysteriously obscure *and* visible, producing secret and manifest, physical as well as moral, effects. All these pairs and ambiguities of meaning are contained in the phrase "the nebula of devotion" as it refers to its historical objects: the various members and activities of the French Resistance.

The lapse of time, and certain permanent (as well as some current) French intellectual dispositions, complicate matters, rendering contemporary access to these important facts even more difficult. There are new mists covering the old ones, and these stars' luster has grown, unfortunately, dimmer with the passing of time. This colloquium, this "necessary exercise of memory" as Mr. Poncelet phrased it, was intended to restore to the French people of all generations a better, because more accurate and more elevating, view of themselves, their country, and their past.

It is my hope that these gripping accounts given in many voices— from that of the dispassionate historian to the active resister, from the grateful American pilot downed in France to the matter-of-fact survivor of the camp at Ellrich—may contribute to bridge the unfortunate gap, the "transatlantic misunderstanding," that too often characterizes Franco-American relations and that, of late, has taken been taken to a dangerous low point.

A final word. I had the good fortune of having preexisting English versions of three of the contributions, Ambassador Vernon

Walters', Arthur L. Funk's, and Ralph Patton's; I made good use of
them. Such inaccuracies and infelicities that remain are my own responsibility.

Paul Seaton

Notes

1.   In my defense, however, I would note that Mrs. Christine Levisse-Touzé begins her
     exposition by noting that the phrase induces "a certain confusion in the reader or
     hearer."
2.   He was a member of the National Council of the Resistance. See the contributions
     of F-G Dreyfus and Mrs. Christine Levisse-Touzé.

Introduction

François-Georges Dreyfus

The colloquium on the "unrecognized resistance" was organized by the Club Témoin, founded in June 1998 by a diverse group (an ambassador, a general, a deputy, a journalist, a Sorbonne professor) who had played an important role in the Resistance, joined by others with State-recognized claims to participation in "the Resistance." They wanted to give personal witness concerning the Occupation, the Resistance, and the deportations, in order to confront a simplistic vision of the history of that dramatic period and to fight against the disinformation that sometimes characterizes the presentation of that sad and painful period of French history.

The Club Témoin wants to underscore the importance of the French Resistance. It maintains that alongside the Resistance of various "movements," of the role of the "networks," one should emphasize the civilian Resistance of the general population. That was the aim of the colloquium which was the origin of this book, a colloquium that took place in the Luxembourg Palace, the seat of the French Senate, under the auspices of its president, Mr. Christian Poncelet. One will see that what made for the richness of this colloquium was the confrontation, rather, the convergence, of French historians (Mrs. Levisse-Touzé, Mr. F-G Dreyfus, professor at the Sorbonne, and Patrick Martin, agrégé of the University) and American ones (Professors John Sweets and Arthur L. Funk) and of famous Americans such as General Vernon Walters and Mr. Ralph Patton, president of the Air Forces Escape and Evasion Society, with famous Frenchmen such as Maurice Delarue and Jacques de Bresson. But "grass-roots" resisters also took part in this conference and their often quite precise testimony was very moving.

*   *   *

1

From 1940 to 1944 France experienced one of the most terrible periods of its history. The French army, poorly prepared by a pacifist political class that was blind to danger and aboulic (that is, lacking will power) since the beginning of the 1930s, and badly commanded by old and conformist generals, was defeated in six weeks (between May 10 and June 25) despite the heroism of its soldiers. (During the French campaign there were as many deaths as during an analogous period during the Battle of Verdun!) The campaign ended with the Armistice of June 25, 1940, which the French Parliament gathered at Vichy in July did not disavow. The Armistice envisaged an occupied zone that would encompass and combine two-thirds of the country. The southern zone, together with Vichy, was the poorest part of France.

The Third Republic fell victim to an absurd political system, which explains the defeat. To it succeeded a new regime, the French State, directed by Marshal Pétain. He was surrounded by individuals hostile to the Third Republic and who came from all points of view: "Young Turks" of the Left, Christian Democrats, moderate Republicans, and monarchists. The Vichy government instituted some very good reforms that have lasted until today and are appreciated. But at the same time it engaged in a policy of rupture with the humanistic traditions that belonged to France since the Ancien Régime and were accentuated by the Revolution, and put in place a State-sponsored anti-Semitism, which issued in the deportation of several tens of thousands of Jews that the Germans exterminated at Auschwitz.

On the diplomatic plane, the Vichy government was traumatized by Churchill's policies, which included attacking the French fleet that had repaired to Algeria at Mers el-Kébir on July 3, 1940, and attempting to take Dakar in September. The government moved closer to the Reich. Marshal Pétain met Hitler in Montoire on October 24, 1940, and agreed "to collaborate" with Germany. But at the same time the Marshal sent an emissary, Professor Rougier, to Churchill. Thus was born a modus vivendi between France and Great Britain that lasted from November 1940 until May 1941.

But the victories of the Wehrmacht led Admiral Darlan, the successor to the germanophile Pierre Laval, in the spring of 1941 to engage for a time in a policy of rapprochement with the Reich, a policy facilitated by the British attack on Syria, then administered by France. Darlan, however, very quickly became aware of his mistake and sought to come closer to the United States, thanks to the activity of the American ambassador, Admiral Leahy. Darlan was replaced by Laval in April 1942. Pierre Laval clearly engaged France in collaboration with the Reich, encouraging the rounding up of foreign Jews and adopting obligatory work service (STO) of the young for Germany. In November 1942, when the Americans and the British landed in North Africa, Marshal Pétain refused to go to Algeria, thinking—and rightly so—that in this way he would avoid the "polandization of France" but in so doing he disserved the higher interests of France. From November 1942 on Philippe Pétain was shunted from power to the advantage of Laval, who immersed himself in collaboration and allowed certain of his minions to engage in abominable operations of repression against the Resistance.

As everyone knows, on June 18, 1940, General de Gaulle, the former aide to Paul Reynaud, "called" upon France and the French to pursue the war. At the beginning he was scarcely heard: hardly 5,000 Frenchmen, officials or soldiers, followed him. Isolated, in order to make himself respected Charles de Gaulle emphasized his intransigence, which explains the difficulties with Churchill and above all with Roosevelt. The latter for a long time only saw in him a sort of South American "caudillo" and preferred the former politicians of the Third Republic to him, especially E. Herriot. Little by little de Gaulle reinforced his position but his power did not really take shape until after the assassination of Admiral Darlan, who commanded in North Africa after the British-American landing, and the reverses of General Giraud, who was rejected by the interior Resistance.

The latter had appeared as early as July 1940. In fact, from that moment the special services of Vichy, with Colonels Rivet and Paillolle, took up the clandestine fight against the Reich. In September 1940 in Marseille, the Movement of National Liberation, started by Captain H. Frenay, was formed. At Montpellier, a Christian-Democrat movement, Liberties, and in the occupied zone, three movements, the Civilian and Military Organization (OCM), Northern Liberation, and Defense of France, were established. A little later, in the southern zone, Liberation and Free Marksman were born. These movements played a great role because, even if they only had some tens of thousands of militants, their propagandistic activity reached hundreds of thousands of French. In 1943 newspapers like *Combat* or *Defense of France* each printed more than 200,000 copies every two weeks.

In June 1941, after having struggled against Vichy and the "Anglo-Gaullist" capitalists, the Communists entered into the resistance and actively engaged in sabotage, but also in assaults on individuals, which accelerated the terrible German repression.

At the same time extraordinarily active information networks were put in place. There were those depending on London that the Central Office of Information and Action (BCRA) established (Confraternity of Notre Dame, the Network of Saint-Jacques, Century), British networks (the Buckmaster Alliance), then after 1942 the American networks, connected with the Office of Strategic Services (OSS).

These movements, after the creation by Vichy of le Service du travail obligatoire (STO), an obligatory work service, encouraged the establishment of the underground, which brought together combatants trained for ambushes and sabotage.

General de Gaulle became aware of the importance of these activities at the beginning of 1942. In order to coordinate them he sent to France Jean Moulin. In eighteen months this indefatigable envoy, infinitely more diplomatic than has been said, united the movements and the networks depending upon them in a National Council of the Resistance (CNR), loyal to de Gaulle. He established work groups to put in place organizations to prepare parachute drops and airplane landing sites, including for the famous DC3s. Hunted by the Gestapo, he was arrested near Lyon in June 1943 and died after terrible torture. But his work lasted and allowed the Resistance to play an important role in the liberation of France (General Eisenhower said, the equivalent of fifteen divisions).

But alongside these movements, these networks, and the underground, there was the unknown Resistance: the person who carried the mail, provided supplies to the underground, helped the "escapes and evasions" of prisoners of war or the repatriation of RAF or U.S. Air Force pilots whose planes had been shot down. They furnished false papers, they harbored by hiding the hunted and persecuted of all sorts: resisters, political opponents, Jews. Here, as Asher Cohen has underscored, Christian churches, priests, pastors, and religious played an important role. But we must not forget the innumerable farmers and "simple" individuals. It was all of them that the Club Témoin called the "unrecognized resistance" and that it wanted to honor by this book.

Message of Mr. Christian Poncelet, President of the French Senate, at the Opening of the Colloquium Dedicated to the "Unrecognized Resistance," Senate, December 4, 2000

Unfortunately retained outside Paris, I nonetheless would like to offer to all those present my warm welcome to the Senate. The Senate is happy to host a colloquium devoted to the "unrecognized resistance."

I would like to compliment my friends Jean Matteoli[1] and Alain Griotteray[2] for the active part they have played, and to thank the numerous foreign dignitaries in attendance, especially Ambassador Vernon Walters, the indefatigable agent of American public and private diplomacy, for their presence.

It is good that a more vivid light is shed upon this "unrecognized resistance" at the service of France and of man. Contrary to legend, the forces of good were active and did not merely await victory. Everywhere, the Resistance was organized. Everywhere, fundamental solidarities allowed some lives to be saved.

The necessary exercise of memory, undertaken with the lapse of time, whether it be a question of the Occupation or of Algeria, often has the effect of rendering one's picture of the event more complex and nuanced, of complicating—"entangling"—or even, sometimes, undoing, the image one had made of it.

Similarly, it is valuable that witnesses come to speak—with the power of their memories, with their faith in our values that still resonates—about what those inspiring struggles were, in order to restore their luster.

For myself, I deeply hope that this colloquium will contribute to the edification of the young and to the prevention of future conflicts.

Notes

1.   Former deputy of the National Assembly; president of the Foundation of the Resistance.
2.   Founder of the Orion network; honorary deputy of the National Assembly.

Presentation by Alain Griotteray, Former Head of the Orion Network

There are certain moments of their long history that the French retain like a sickness. It took them two centuries to work up the courage to treat the war of the Vendée and its massacres as they should. Up until the two hundredth anniversary of the Revolution it was a war one was not to speak about, one that was barely mentioned in the history books. And yet how much courage, hope, and freedom, and how many noble passions, confronted one another in those terrible battles!

Take another tragedy from which we have not extricated ourselves: the Paris Commune of 1871. For a long time the arguments from Versailles prevailed. Then little by little, it was "the wall of the Federals" that became a national symbol. And it is the book *The Time of Strawberries* (that charming catchphrase) that has remained in our hearts and on our lips!

The sacrifices of the War of 1914-1918, the unimaginable number of deaths, the sufferings of all the generations have effaced all the wounds that, there too, could have left painful scars.

Exhausted by its sacrifices, and because of the mediocrity of the end of the Third Republic, France experienced another tragedy, the lost battle of May-June 1940, despite the hundred thousand dead who are already forgotten by history. And the long night of the Occupation and then the Liberation. Only then did the French give themselves over to heartfelt joy. Since the Liberation, though, the propaganda of the Communists, those who at the time had approved the German-Soviet pact but because of the German attack against Russia reversed their stance, placing their courage, sacrifices, and facility for clandestine operations until the end of the Reich at the service of our struggle, created a politicized legend: all the French were resisters except for the bourgeoisie and the Right. Then there

7

was *The Sorrow and the Pity* (a film on the Resistance): "All the French had been cowards and more or less collaborators."

And the new generations no longer know what to believe. When a weekly [publication] dares to splash a title like, "Finally, the truth," one almost could believe that the wicked, the traitors, were not punished. The truth is that for the first time in history, even if scapegoats often had to pay, the most important leaders were judged, condemned, and shot. Marshal Pétain was not executed, but only because of his old age...and our allies. The others—Laval, Brinon, Darnad, to name only a few—were shot after questionable trials. To be sure, it is commonly agreed that there were heroes: those of the Free French who joined General de Gaulle from 1940. It is agreed that there were resisters, that there were networks of information and then of action, great "movements" of resistance also, which grew little by little in 1943-1944. There was Jean Moulin and the National Council of the Resistance (CNR). Before that, there had been the struggle of emblematic heroes such as Honoré d'Estienne d'Orves and his comrades, who were condemned to death and executed at a time when the war had not yet taken the atrocious turn of massive deportations and the installation in France of the Gestapo (whose 1944 Paris heads, Oberg and Knochen, died in their beds in Germany after the war. But that belongs to the history of the Germans.).

The founding president of the Club Témoin, Ambassador A. Chambon (1909-2002), took upon himself the task of making known how the French people in its entirety lived through the defeat, the Occupation, and the great hopes of Gaullism. There were heroes, as I said. The greatest detractors of our country acknowledge as much. There were rotters and scoundrels. There always are rotters when a country suffers a defeat and is occupied by the enemy. There also were the administrators of the defeat. It is not the intention of the Club nor of this colloquium to attend to them. No, what the Club wants to bring to light and make known is the conduct of the usually voiceless, of the people dazed by the defeat, by the number of prisoners, the people subject to enemy propaganda. On all the walls lovely posters declared: "Frenchmen, trust the German soldiers." Well, they didn't give them their trust.

To be sure, my friend Henri Amouroux is right to have written "that in the summer of 1940 there were forty million Pétainists." But what does that mean? That the French, the Belgians, and the Dutch, who were subject on the open road to the strafings of the Stukas, thought that one must stop the fight, that all the refugees ought to return home, that a great people doesn't die on exposed roads, and that Marshal Pétain was right to sign the Armistice. But an armistice is no more "peace" than mobilization is "war."

Then came the winter of 1940, the coldest that France had known in a long time. The shortages. Parisians had not yet reconnected with their country cousins to give them a little food. The winter was terrible. It was marked however by the birth of the networks, as I can testify. The Franco-Belgian Chain of Henri d'Astier de la Vigerie and of Georges Piron took its risks in the interallied zone, providing information on the German preparations for landing in England. But it was also marked by that demonstration, due to the instinct of the young, that united high school and college students in order to carry the cross of Lorraine on the sacred flagstone to the Étoile. It was some thousands of youth who, from three o'clock to six o'clock, confronted the surprised Germans.

Igor de Schotten, the president of the Alumni of November 11, 1940, recalled that the indulgent French police helped the students to go up to the tomb of the unknown soldier and place a cross of Lorraine on the sacred flagstone. But the German army mixed in. The youth arrested by the French police were taken to the Champs Élysées-Clemenceau police station and were freed during the night. In contrast, those who had been taken by the Germans spent some weeks in prison at Cherche-Midi or Fresnes.

General de Gaulle declared that this was the first response he received from the people of Paris. And the other day Pierre Messmer evoked his memories of Africa in 1940 for us, at the gathering to commemorate the sixtieth anniversary of November 11, 1940, in these words: "We Free French, cut off from France, were without news. When the radio informed us about the demonstration of November 11, we found great comfort in it. In Paris young French were partners in our fight."

Of that little is said. In truth, if all the men of the Isle of Sein joined General de Gaulle in 1940, it was because it was possible for them, it was easy! For Parisian students it was a different matter. It wasn't until the end of 1942 to the beginning of 1943, when the free zone was occupied in its turn, that from the Spanish side came help. Up until November 1942, the Spanish returned those trying to escape to the Vichy police. From the moment when the Germans controlled the border, they never delivered an escapee to the Germans.

To be sure, the "Spanish misadventure" (to use the expression of Lucien Bodard[1]) includes the prisons, but there were twenty thousand young people who joined the French armies of the Liberation in North Africa via Spain.

My own network, the Orion network, just celebrated the courage of the inhabitants of St.-Jean-Pied-de-Port with a plaque. That plaque expressed the gratitude of those wanting to escape for the courage of those who sheltered and assisted them and helped them to cross the border at the risk of their own lives. Some who aided them were executed or deported. These were the French—some say, the "disengaged, wait-and-see" French—of the Occupation. Disengaged, too, were the monks of the abbey of Belloc. And there, too, with abbé Maurice Cordier, president of the Escaped from France via Spain, we have erected a memorial stone, a symbol of the gratitude of all those who passed through there to find the path of escape. The Father Abbot and the Father Prior were arrested by the Gestapo in 1943 and deported. I rarely cite Mao Tse-Tung, but here I willingly reprise his saying, "The revolutionary, in order to be effective, must move like a fish in water." This was the case for us resisters. If we hadn't been surrounded by "a current of sympathy, a mist of sympathy, a nebula of devotion and sacrifice..." according to the extraordinary formulation of Debû-Bridel.[2]

It is this surrounding current of devotion and sacrifice that the Club Témoin intends to recall today in order to put to an end the masochistic legends of those who always want to sully France. Children and young people ought to know the courageous conduct of their elders.

The Club Témoin has worked in association with the Hoover Institution, one of the most prestigious American universities. François-Georges Dreyfus, whose contribution to the historiography of those times is universally recognized, has brought together with him French and American historians. The Americans come to hear our accounts and to testify themselves to what they have learned during the course of their work.

We have with us Arthur L. Funk of the University of Florida, president of the American Committee of the History of the Second World War, and John Sweets, who taught at Duke University, then the University of Kansas, also consultant at the universities of Dublin and Besançon. Also among us is General Walters, whose career has earned him every decoration in the world and in particular ours, a former ambassador, he knows Europe better than anyone. Finally, beside these eminent professors and dignitaries, is Ralph Patton, president of the Association of Escaped American Aviators, an organization for those who were helped to escape the Germans by anonymous French men and women. He will talk about his own experiences, but he brings with him the cases of all the members of his association who escaped thanks to "the anonymous," those whom no one will decorate and who sometimes were not even thanked.

Since I open this colloquium, I will recount one of my own experiences. When I returned a second time to territory occupied by the enemy, my mission was organized by the OSS. I parachuted from a "flying fortress" into the Atlantic side of the Pyrenees at Orion, a small village of three hundred souls that, in 1941, gave its name to my network. No one was expecting me. I had preferred to add to my risks during the night rather than to alert a welcoming committee, which often gave rise to indiscretions, then arrests. My network had been shaken, like others, during my absence. Arrests and deportations had occurred, but also escapes, including escapes from deportation trains.

I found myself not too far from the meadow I had chosen but unfortunately in a wood. I was lost. I learned that day that the most precise compass (which the Americans had given me) does no good if one doesn't know where one is or where one is going! I walked, therefore, without ever crossing or retracing my steps, and I, fatefully, arrived at a road not far from a farm. The dogs were barking. A light shed its light by a window that was opened. I am a friend of the masters of the chateau, I said. (There were good and there were bad chateaux, however.) But the peasant had heard the noise of the airplane and asked me right away, "Ah, are you from the airplane that just went away? Don't move, I'm coming."

That man never would have "resisted" if my path hadn't crossed his. He guided me through the wood and also found my parachute, which had made a great white splotch, a striking sign for the Luftwaffe when it would survey the region the next day. He helped me, even when I was ready to postpone the search for later, to recover my equipment dropped by another parachute. And then he harbored me, hid me, and alerted my accomplices at the chateau. In fact, only a few accomplices remained. Only two sisters of "a certain age." Mrs. Labbé, little aware of what her son, Paul, and I had undertaken at Orion and elsewhere the past three years. In fact, she had just learned of the death in combat of Paul. Her other older son had been killed in 1940. She and her sister, Miss Reclus, immediately adopted me and a few days later I regained Paris.

The unrecognized resistance, that's it. I benefited from it. And if I am here, opening this colloquium today, it is thanks to her. To that resistance that some have wanted to erase from our memory. But I, I spoke French, I was known to the village. The American aviators shot down over France knew next to nothing about the country in which they had fallen. Ralph Patton will tell us how he extricated himself—or was extricated. In fact, the various books that bear witness all say the same thing. The memoirs of an agent of Free France, Colonel Rémi,[3] those of Marie-Madeleine Fourcade, the head of the Alliance network, and so many others, of Passy, head of the BCRA, of Colonel Amoud, head of Jade-Amical, if one wants to read them, they contain the same message about all these "disengaged, wait-and-see" French, about the unrecognized resistance that surrounded them.

It seems, however, that a certain type of historian doesn't read them. Better put, he ignores them. And sometimes he attains an absolute ignorance. Journalists do not even make a distinction between 1940 and 1943-1944. I remember having been invited by Mrs. Christine Ockrent[4] to a television show in order to help young people learn about the history of the Occupation. I recounted how, at the end of 1940, I crossed the line of demarcation for the first time. Why had I, a Parisian, tried my luck at Orthez, I no longer know. I had an address, no doubt. No doubt, I thought that a Parisian would be less expected at the other end of France than at the line of demarcation at Moulin, or even closer to Paris. I therefore had an address, that of an inn where an older woman (she had to be forty years old) gave me food and shelter. She made me an exceptional meal, one that a Parisian such as myself had not known in several months. Then in the night she entrusted me to a man (an "old" man, who had to be twenty-five—please remember that I was eighteen!) who was my first guide. At the time of my departure the lady said to her husband, "Give him some money, he is so young and he will need some there where he is going." There where he is going! She knew where I wanted to go. Arrived as anticipated at the border of the "no-no"(non-occupied) zone, I stopped at the station of the gendarmes, who received me in a quite friendly way, gave me breakfast, and wished me good luck!

At this point Christine Ockrent interrupted me: "But there were the militia?" "No, Madame, the militia were in 1944!"

In the audience, no one supported me. No, one did. Professor Rémond of the French Academy came to my aid. It was a surprise to me, but it was true: barely older than I, he had been a member of Free France.

This morning we are going to try to bring this unrecognized resistance to view and make it better known.

France is really something other than this furious determination to disparage itself that regularly takes hold of the French, the press, and the pundits. Once again we are living through one of these deplorable moments. Maurice Druon of the French Academy just wrote a pamphlet, "France at the Command of a Cadaver." The cadaver is the Soviet Union. It is, alas, still living among us. Look at the way in which a campaign is underway to show the culpability of the French army in North Africa. Yet one may observe today the way in which the Algerians slaughter one another. Every day we hear on the radio and we read in the press the account of children murdered a few kilometers from Algiers, in the south to east of Algiers, or somewhere in Algeria. That was the method they used against us at the time: first against the French; then, since that did not suffice, against the heads of villages, friends of France; and then, since that did not always suffice, in order to show that the French no longer could protect the population, they slaughtered the women and children of their race just as they do today the children. It is Boutéflika[5] who ought to ask forgiveness.

If someone is responsible, if someone is culpable, it is the Communists who were accomplices in the Algerian rebellion. The Algerian Communist Party that delivered bombs designed to assassinate.

The goal of this propaganda is to make one believe that the French were complicitous with the Germans. Some have even wanted to make them guilty of the Holocaust. God forbid, here too the unrecognized resistance touched the Jews. A Jewish historian, Asher Cohen, in a monumental volume (which isn't always kind toward us) explains why the percentage (oh, the horrible word!) of Jewish victims in France was less than all the other countries occupied by Germany. This book, which renders homage to the unrecognized resistance, is unfortunately little known, and it is almost impossible to find. I recommend it to you. Its title is: *Persecution and Rescue in France: Jews under the Occupation*.[6]

All the members of the Club Témoin have at heart the desire to "bear witness" (from the French, *témoin*. Trans.). Ambassador Chambon brought together in the Club all types, those who were deported, resisters, and Free French, those who were agents and witnesses. And also the youngest, the generation immediately after ours, whose most brilliant member is François-Georges Dreyfus, then other young people. This was done so that in their turn, when the eyewitnesses have passed on, they can make known to others our experiences, the unrecognized resistance.

There are other subjects to be treated, to be sure. The Armistice, Vichy, Gaullism, the latent civil war, the purging. These belong to other histories. This morning I conclude by saying that in an occupied country there will always be "Bishop Cochons."[7] Perhaps the only crime of a people is to lose a war, because when one loses a war one incurs the risk of also losing one's soul. Then there are the "Bishop Cochons" who collaborate. But there are also the Joans of Arc. Must I tell you that I am forever on the side of Joan of Arc, she who could not have fulfilled her mission except with God's assistance? She too needed, and found, the unrecognized resistance of a people surrounding her who aspired to liberty and independence, like the French people of 1940 to 1945.

Notes

1.   A journalist and great reporter (F-G Dreyfus' note).
2.   J. Debû-Bridel, writer and journalist, was member of the National Council of the Resistance.
3.   Founder and head of one of the most important networks of information, the Confraternity of Notre Dame.
4.   Hostess on the television channel, France 2, and wife of a government minister.
5.   President of the Algerian Republic.
6.   *Persécution et sauvetage en France: les Juifs sous l'Occupation* (Éditions du Cerf, 1995).
7.   An allusion to Bishop Cochon, who presided over the tribunal at Rouen that condemned Joan of Arc to death.

Studies

What was the Resistance?

François-Georges Dreyfus

For the past thirty years the Resistance has occupied a consider-able place in the historiography of France. But that has lead both French and non-French historians to write sometimes very question-able pages.[1] It appears necessary to recall certain essential facts that too often are ignored.

1. On June 25, 1940 the war ceased on the French front after a terrible and tragic defeat. At the time of the Armistice, Lyon, Nevers, and Poitiers were in the hands of the Wehrmacht, which was also at the gates of Grenoble, of Clermont-Ferrand, and of Bordeaux. Cal-culating on the basis of the advance of the German armies between the 10th of June and the 23rd, Bordeaux and Marseille would have been occupied before the end of the month. Was it necessary to continue the war? General de Gaulle, with courage, intelligence, and determination, called for the continuation of fighting. But with what means? There no longer was a land army, except for certain units here and there. The almost entirely intact navy remained as well as very diminished aerial forces: there were six hundred modern air-planes in Algeria, but they lacked replacement parts and ammuni-tion; moreover their outfitting wasn't complete.

As General Guderian notes, it only took the Wehrmacht a few days to cross Spain and attack Morocco. Now, the French divisions of North Africa prepared for combat were on the Libyan-Tunisian border on the Mareth line; to confront Morocco, General Noguès only had two divisions. He asked for six more in order to remain in the field: no one could furnish them; there no longer was an English army.

François-Georges Dreyfus is professor emeritus of contemporary history at the Sorbonne (Paris-IV), and has also taught history and political science at the IEP de Paris and the Institut für Europaïsche Geschichte à Mayence. He is the author of several books, including *De Gaulle et le Gaullisme*, *Histoire de la Démocratie-chrétienne en France*, *Histoire de la Résistance*, and *Histoire de Vichy*.

Moreover, one might think that the Luftwaffe, certainly supported by Italian aviation, could have, if not prevented, at least strongly bothered the passage of the fleet from Toulon to Bizert or Mers el-Kébir, especially if—as General Franco proposed to Hitler on the 16th of June—Spain lent bases to the Reich.

Objectively speaking, therefore, to ask for an armistice wasn't irrational. But as General Weygand will immediately say, "an armistice isn't peace"; in his eyes it was necessary to act like the Reich itself in 1918. The problem is that that was not the way the government of Vichy would react.

2. The armistice divided France into several zones. Let us simply distinguish the occupied zone and the so-called "free zone," the southern zone.

In the occupied zone the Wehrmacht was quite present; at certain times there were close to two million men in these regions. The population felt it physically and daily and suffered the consequences: requisition of houses, the seizure of foodstuffs, obtrusive control by the administration. A passive resistance very quickly developed, sometimes even active (the cutting of telephone cables, railway sabotage), but that remained rare until the spring of 1941; networks of information and aid also appeared, for those seeking to escape German capture (the networks Museum of Man, Northern Liberation, the Civilian and Military Organization: OCM), which quickly enough envisaged the establishment of armed groups.

In the southern zone, the situation in 1940 was totally different: Marshal Pétain was the object of adulation (cf. Cardinal Gerlier's, Archbishop of Lyon, declaration: "Pétain is France, France is Pétain.") even if his government was sharply criticized. December 13, 1940, the day of a coup d'état against Laval, the government's "ratings" received a boost. One only has to read the Manifesto that H. Frenay[2] circulated to launch the first Movement of national liberation; he defended the Marshal and even is not hostile to the get-together at Montoire. It is true—and this is too frequently forgotten—that Marshal Pétain at the same time sent Professor Rougier, who was a personal friend of Lord Halifax, to London in order to negotiate with Churchill a modus vivendi concerning the blockade, in exchange for Vichy non-intervention in the AEF. The accord was in place from November 1940 until May 1941. At that time there truly was a double game being played.

To be sure, in addition to Frenay's movement—which called it-self for a time "the Little Wings" and published a bulletin—other groups appeared: those of a popular democratic character around P. H. Teitgen, Capitant, and F. de Menthon (all three professors of pub-lic law); Liberties would meld with Frenay's movement to become Combat, later connected with the leftist Free Marksmen of J. P. Levy and Liberation of E. d'Astier de la Vigerie. These four movements—and some others that were strictly local—never contained more than three to four thousand people at the absolute most. And some mem-bers, such as Toulousans in the spring of 1941, counted as members of each one of them. As for the others, the police were generally good-natured and they attached hardly any importance locally to what were in the main only small groups. In a city such as Montpellier in June 1941 there were not even eighty resisters, of which two-thirds were professors (Marc Bloch, P. H. Teitgen) or students at the University.[3]

In contrast, the hunt for Communists was active and brutal. But then they acted as revolutionaries, not as resisters. For them, de Gaulle, as well as Pétain, was a lackey of capitalism. More or less protected by the Germans in the occupied zone, they were actively sought in the southern zone. The small fry went to prison, the higher-ups were captured and interrogated or most often transferred to southern Al-geria—which allowed them to avoid deportation to Germany.

3. It was in the springtime of 1941 that the situation changed. Convinced of a Germany victory, Admiral Darlan, the vice-presi-dent of the Council, entered into a policy of rupture with London and of collaboration with the Reich, going so far as to sign (at the end of May 1941) the Protocols of Paris, which would have made France de facto an ally of Germany. But Marshal Pétain, supported by General Weygand,[4] firmly opposed the document and it was never applied.

June 22, 1941, the Reich invaded the Soviet Union. The next day the Communist Party entered the Resistance. They also modified its features. The first movements manufactured propaganda, provided information, helped prisoners of war and pilots of the RAF get to the borders and avoid capture. The Communist Resistance wanted to attack directly the occupying forces (assaults against the leaders or the strongholds of the Wehrmacht, sabotage) and they based them-selves on a militarized organization, the Free Marksmen and Parti-sans (FTP). This strategy that was imposed by Moscow was tragic. It hardly affected the Wehrmacht. From June 1941 to March 1944 the Wehrmacht lost less than 2,500 men because of the Resistance (out of a minimum of one million soldiers, that is, 0.25 percent) but over 10,000 men because of vehicle accidents. German reprisals, on the other hand, entailed for the same period close to 10,000 people shot and around 50,000 deported (the resisters who were deported are not separated here). The Communist strategy was even more damaging as it pushed non-Communist organizations to analogous actions that were very costly in lives for singularly limited results. One will recall that General de Gaulle condemned the attacks, but he cried in the desert. Later Colonel Passy, head of the Special Services of Free France, criticized the policy of the FTP that their head, P. Villon, had conveyed to him.

Whatever the Communist Party may have thought, these attacks had barely any resonance in the general population which, "in the mass," noted Colonel Reile, head of the Abwehr in France, "was relatively indifferent." He coldly added: "Moreover, factories continue to run regularly, even those that work for the Reich." I note that if there was a general coalmining strike in May 1941, there were no strikes from June 1941 to June 1944 in the metallurgy that made or repaired trucks, tanks, cannons, and planes for the Wehrmacht, nor any strikes of railwaymen. In the fight against the Communists, in March 1942 the Reich demoted the military and the Abwehr and installed the SS, commanded by an Oberführer. The repression was going to become terribly brutal.

4. 1942 marked a turning point in the life of France, in particular in the southern zone.

In the northern zone the anti-Semitic campaign began in December 1941 and attained its peak with the roundup of "the Vel. d'hiv" of July 1942: twelve thousand foreign Jews were rounded up and would be sent to Auschwitz.

In the southern zone P. Laval, who had had the statute on Jews adopted on October 3, 1940, and who replaced Admiral Darlan in April 1942, in August 1942 ordered the return to the Reich of twenty thousand foreign Jewish refugees found in the southern zone, often in camps put in place by the government of the Republic in 1939.

In addition Laval authorized the German police to locate the radio transmitters of the Resistance in the free zone and to operate against the resisters. All that contributed to turn upside-down the

behavior of the French in the southern zone, which was in the process of dramatically changing in May 1942, as a synthesis of reports
of prefects to the Minister of the Interior in May 1942 makes clear:

> The British aggression against Madagascar did not publicly have the resentment [sic] of
> disapproval stated by the press. The common view is that certain of the more salient
> demonstrations were organized.
>
> It's enough to rub shoulders with "the man in the street" to take stock of his state of
> mind:
>
> • He accepts with resignation the British assaults on our colonial empire. He ex-
> plains them as necessary for England in order to deny Germany the use of our colonies;
>
> • He is pleased with the difficulties experienced by the Axis troops in Russia. He
> hopes that the Soviets and the Nazis do each other enough damage that they no longer
> are dangerous;
>
> • He doesn't hide his joy at the announcement of a German reverse, no matter how
> small;
>
> • He is irritated when the French radio or press report events that foreign radios
> communicated several days before. He believes himself shut off;
>
> • He is troubled by the lot reserved for prisoners and one perhaps should see in this
> anxiousness the real reason for the apparent passivity of the population;
>
> • He recognizes plainly that the Marshal saved France from a situation that seemed
> hopeless, but he has the feeling that governmental decisions are either inspired by Nazi
> policy or dictated by the Chancellor of the Reich.
>
> In short, the "average" Frenchman
> —is anti-German;
> —trusts Marshal Pétain.

In June 1942 the "matter of the relief force" occurred, the prelude
to the STO (obligatory work service in Germany), which in turn
occasioned the establishment of the underground. Finally, the landing in North Africa of November 8, 1942 accelerated the course of
events. Marshal Pétain, despite the objections of General Weygand
and numerous ministers including Jean Borotra and François
Lehideux, decided to remain in France because he thought
thereby to better protect the interests of the French. But his decision seems to have been contrary to those of France. It is clear that
the entrance of France into war with a prestigious leader, a reno-
vated air force, and an almost intact fleet would have given it a place
in the war (and later in the peace that followed) that it unfortunately
will not have.[5]

For the majority of French opinion, November 1942 was the turning point in as much as from then on the entire country was occupied.

5. It was then that the undergrounds appeared. They "represent
more than a simple military phenomenon." But until the beginning
of 1944 the undergrounds were almost uniquely a feature of the

southern zone, because in the northern zone they would have been more difficult to establish, due to German surveillance.

The German military arrangements in the southern zone were infinitely more lax. There was in this a fundamental strategic element: After November 8, 1942 the OKW knew that there would be a landing in the west and it was convinced that it would take place on the Channel coast, somewhere between Dunkirk and Cherbourg. Hence the collection on the Atlantic side of the essential northern forces in a line: Poitiers-Dijon-Belfort. Of thirty-six operational divisions, twenty-eight were in this sector, while the Mediterranean sector only had eight divisions, including the 9th Panzer and six infantry divisions whose inadequacies A. L. Funk has demonstrated.[6] There also was a division at Clermont-Ferrand. If one uses the German sources, the essential axes for the Germans in the southern zone were Bordeau-Hendaye, Bordeaux-Nice, Chalons-Lyon, Marseille, and Lons-le-Saunier-Lyons; the rest was not essential.

In fact, the essential sabotage activity took place along secondary lines (e.g., Toulouse-Limoges) or even less than secondary (Béziers-Neussargues). The stopping of the traffic on these lines that served to replenish certain garrisons only had a limited effect on German strategy or tactics and only a secondary importance was attached to it, except when these lines served the transportation of useful basic materials (e.g., bauxite). Those who were really interested were the affected garrisons, and it was their small active units who responded. At no time did the division of "operational" infantry at Montpellier really take action against the underground. It was the mobile elements of the garrisons of Nîmes and Montpellier who acted, i.e., units at the battalion level of around 500 men (although, it is true, disposing of means of combat very superior to those of the underground: light armor, field artillery, mortars, and machine guns).

We know today from a report of the Militärbefehlshaber that in May 1944 the Wehrmacht had deployed (for the entirety of France):

One Schnellverband (rapid deployment formation) of two battalions and one detachment of reconnaissance;
   Seven security battalions, of which three lacked heavy arms;
   Seven battalions drawn from the forces.

Fourteen battalions is about 10,000 men and the Schnellverband, 2,000. In all, for the entirety of France about 12,000 men, barely a division, of which 7,000 were not intended for the Atlantic front.

Opposing them, in December 1943—and this gives an idea of the means the underground possessed in March 1944—the undergrounds could field, according to the report of the Military Action Commission (COMIDAC):

Unified Movements of the Resistance	MUR	FTP
Northern zone	14,000	7,000
Southern zone	13,800	5,000
Totals	27,800	12,000[7]

But these men hardly had rifles or machine guns. Moreover, against the Glières, the Wehrmacht deployed less than 4,000 men of the 157th Alpine reserve division—whose deployment in the west was never envisaged—and 1,000 militia men, accompanied, it is true, by twenty-four tanks and sixteen cannons, then on thinking about it, two battalions of infantry, one regiment of artillery, and one large squadron of tanks.

In fact, the actions of the undergrounds, even if they irritated the Germans they hardly vexed them, and they hardly helped the Allies. They had only a secondary utility. An argument of G. Bouladou in his *Hérault in the Resistance* is very significant: In June and July 1944 the rail lines Bédarieux-Castres, Millau-Bédarieux, and Béziers-Lodève were sabotaged. They were rendered unusable for periods ranging from six hours to four days. During this period, quite obviously, it was not these lines that interested the Wehrmacht, but rather the main Bordeaux-Marseille via Bèziers Sète and Montpellier. And it took serious bombardments at Sète and Montpellier, causing numerous civilian casualties, to stop its traffic for thirty hours. All that explains the Koenig-Eisenhower accord concerning aerial bombardments, an accord that continues to scandalize many resisters and some historians. The case of the departments of Languedoc is typical. The small lines were sabotaged, while the major ones were hardly touched, to the point that on August 17, two days after the landing in Provence, resisters kept in the Saint-Michel prison of Toulouse were deported by train to Germany! It was the same for the high officials and notable inhabitants of Languedoc. They were arrested by the Gestapo in June 1944 and immediately deported! Finally, the XI Panzer would be transferred without any real difficulty from Bor-

deaux to Toulouse at the beginning of August, then between August
15 and 19 from Toulouse to Avignon!

These were the limits of the undergrounds.

One has to underscore the importance of the impact of the STO
(obligatory work service in Germany) on recruitment. Statistics un-
derline that réfractaires (those fleeing work service. Trans.) were
small in number until May 31, 1943. Of the 490,000 conscripted
from June 1, 1942 to March 31, 1943, there were in fact 446,521
deported: not even 10 percent insubordination. It was from the end
of March 1943 that the refusal was clear and obvious: 350,000 requisitioned, 141,000 deported. In general, by the end of August 1943
there were around 250,000 réfractaires. But as we have seen, there
were not 40,000 members of the underground and all were not requisitioned by the STO. It appears that only a little more than 10 percent of the disobedient joined the underground. This is what, in 1978,
the historian P. Silvestre nicely showed concerning the Dauphiné.

Until the spring of 1943 the underground was composed in part
of foreign refugees in flight, who sought a safe haven. The case of
Fred Plisner, a young Austrian Jewish refugee protected by the mayor
of his Cevenole community, is clear enough. It was these who, often
characterized by Marxism and anti-fascism, a few months later would
set the tone in certain undergrounds and contribute to politicizing
them. It is true that the undergrounds, for the most part on the Left,
rather than tactical action too often sought to unleash a revolutionary "coming to consciousness" that did not occur, except in very
rare instances. But this attitude explains certain demands that took
place at the Liberation and afterwards. It also explains the disap-
pointment of the men of certain undergrounds (generally members
of the FTP, but also of the AS) at the successive dissolutions of the
FFI, whose members were integrated in the army from the beginning of September, then of the so-called popular militia.

The action of many of the undergrounds was certainly heroic but
it was of little effect. The XI Panzer stationed at Bordeaux between
August 10 and 19 was able to rejoin, essentially by train and without
almost any difficulty, the Avignon region and seriously hamper the
allied offensive in the Rhône valley. One was not able, or did not
know how, to sabotage the main line, Bordeaux-Marseille, which
was bordered by zones that contained important undergrounds...in
the Black Mountain, for example, the Corbières and the Minervois!
Some insist on the influence of the Caïman plan formulated by the

general staff in Algeria in the Mount Mouchet "affair" in the Massif Central. In reality it was badly conceived and came too late. Even if similar ideas were circulating in the Resistance from the end of the winter of 1944, the plan was not official until May 16, 1944, while the decisions concerning Mount Mouchet were taken in February. To be sure, the Caïman plan was quite conceivable. Nonetheless, by officially bringing out this plan on May 16, 1944, three weeks before the landing, the CFLN and its major staffs showed that they had understood nothing concerning what the role of the undergrounds could be. The central idea of the plan was to cut the lines of retreat of the German forces and to encourage the establishment of three zones of action in the Massif Central.

This required extensive preparations: to mark out the possibilities of surveillance of the access points (which was only superficially done, and hence the surprise caused by the German attack during the attack on Mount Mouchet), and an organized mobilization (which was effective, even if there wasn't the expected mass rising). Above all, there needed to be a global preparation at the level of London or Algeria, sending heavy arms (bazookas, mortars, heavy machine guns) and allied cadres. In reality, the SHAEF did not want to plan a strategy based upon the undergrounds, because people distrusted their Marxist ideology and also General de Gaulle was distrusted. Above all, people were distrustful of any action of the partisans.

Now, a large mobilization, but to the north of Clermont-Ferrand, well prepared, accompanied by the parachute dropping of heavy arms, but also of commandos and air-borne troops, could have seriously bothered the back lines of the German troops from [attending to] the Normandy front. Did people fail to think of that or did they not want to think about it? Really, only Rundstedt thought of it, and that would be the terrible mission of the SS division, Das Reich. In any case, that would have justified rejecting the absurdly useless "immediate action," which was so costly in lives.

In reality, the undergrounds only played a truly strategic role in two very circumscribed zones: Brittany and the quadrilateral, Lyon-Chamonix-Nice-Marseille, in the context of the landing.

Why the landing in Provence? To consider their arrangements, it was in Languedoc that the Germans awaited the Allies. There they stationed four "normal" divisions (the 271, 272, 277, and 338), while between Marseille and Nice there were two "limited employment" divisions (the 242 and 244) and a "reserve" division (the 148). On their side, the Allies hesitated for a long time. In twenty pages, Colonel Gaujac sketches a very suggestive list of the Anglo-American, Franco-American, and Franco-French "controversies."[8] Concerning the role of Anvil (the code name for the Provence landing), one should recall that in mid-February 1944 some had thought of abandoning the Normandy landing for one in Provence. Others, Churchill and the British, thought of a double offensive in Italy and in Yugoslavia, to which Juin agreed but de Gaulle and de Lattre—for once in agreement—rejected.

The interallied Strategic Committee (CCS) finally decided on a landing on the coasts of Provence with strong French participation. The interallied strategic planning foresaw the taking of Toulon at D + 20, Marseille at D + 40, while de Lattre proposed a plan with the taking of Toulon at D + 10. The latter almost perfectly conformed to reality, since Toulon fell at D + 13 and Marseille at D + 12.

In this context the interior Resistance, backed by the Jedburgh teams and supported by allied parachute drops of arms, played the role assigned to it. To be sure, it was sorely tried by the zeal of the Marseilles Gestapo, but also by the absurdity of the instructions from SHAEF for the night of June 5-6. The generalized guerilla warfare at the time fragmented the undergrounds that were supposed to help the disembarked troops. One of the heads of the interior Resistance, Sapin, was consternated by the orders from London: "I don't believe my eyes; twelve days have passed since June 6 and we cannot erase everything and start over, nor, alas, resurrect the dead. We exposed ourselves, we were 'compromised,' and no one saw why the Germans would not have acted as if nothing had happened." Valréas in Vaucluse, "liberated June 8," was overrun on the 10th by the Wehrmacht: there were fifty executions; in Bouches-du-Rhône, two hundred men disappeared in fifteen days.

In contrast, in the Basses and Hautes-Alpes the ORA[9] was able to bring together and arm 6,700 men who would allow the "Combat Command" of the American Seventh army to march on Grenoble and to liberate southern Dauphiné in a few days.

As for the other undergrounds, if they sabotaged the production of bauxite, they only succeeded in "blocking the trains for around ten hours."

In all, the FFI of R2 received seventeen tons of explosives, five 574 Sten machine guns, four 415 rifles, two hundred and eighty-nine FMs, and twenty-two mortars; Vaucluse and the Basses and

Hautes-Alpes took the lion's part with 72 percent of the machine guns, 76 percent of the rifles, and 80 percent of the FMs. The Gard, so much studied by a number of historians, only received 5.5 percent of the machine guns, 9.35 percent of the rifles, 7.6 percent of the FMs, and 7 percent of the explosives: obviously, the Gard didn't interest the Allies; it didn't enter into their strategic field. The small number of parachute drops is not so much due—no matter what some say—to the political affiliations of the resisters as to the place they were thought to hold in the unfolding of the landing campaign. The FFI and too many historians have never wanted to admit that.

In summary, even if this hardly gratifies, one must admit that the undergrounds only played a secondary role in the Resistance, even if they brought together 235,000 voluntary combatants.

6. As we have shown in the *History of the Resistance*,[10] then in *The Patriotism of the French under the Occupation*,[11] the action and activity of Resistance was infinitely more than the 235,000 combatants of the undergrounds and the networks: it brings together all those who participated in one way or another in what J. Debû-Bridel called the "unrecognized resistance."

The "unrecognized resistance" brings together those who, from the beginning, collaborated with the networks of French SRs who did not stop fighting against Germany, the networks of the BCRA of General de Gaulle, of the DGSS of the Committee of Algeria, of the Intelligence Service, and the OSS. Now, all of that combines to make thousands of people. Among them, think of the 7th column of Alsace directed by Dungler and P. Winter who organized, with the financial aid of Marshal Pétain, in fact close to one hundred thousand escapes and evasions, including that of General Giraud and his associates, which was the work of thousands of anonymous individuals.[12]

Let us also consider that alongside the combatant and the information gatherer, there were the scouts who "explored" the entrances of tunnels, who sought "a flat terrain, very clear and withdrawn, about two hundred and fifty meters long and eighty wide," whose reports joined the dossiers of services preparing parachute drops without asking for a second the reason for the question they were answering. There were also the farmers who fed the members of the underground or who hid the politically persecuted or the Jews, and the priests, pastors, and the religious who aided and protected the persecuted Jews. Also among them were those, from the café owner to the gendarme, who helped others get across the line of demarcation or cross the Pyrenees or get to Switzerland. Let's not forget the officials, whether high up or lower down, who managed not to see the hunted, to furnish him with false papers, those gendarmes who didn't "see" a demonstration on December 11 at the monument to the dead in a city in the Drôme, or who ignored the parachute drop zones, or who very quietly hid arms, as in Morbihan. Also, resisters were those who inspired the dramatic productions of "Men at Work," which prepared the youth to serve, first in the forestage, then in the First army.

Very symptomatic in this regard—even if it is on another plane—was the debate between Antoine de Saint-Exupéry and (an astonishingly intolerant) Jacques Maritain. The former called for "union" and inviting people to strike out for Algeria, while Maritain opposed that view in the name of defending an ideal that he thought Free France misunderstood. All this allows us to better understand what the unrecognized resistance was. It unites all those who, from 1940 or from 1942, understood "where" France was and how it was best to serve her. And those were in the millions: without them it is not certain that the victory of the Allies would have been assured.

Notes

1.   Permit me to refer to my two books: *Histoire de la Résistance* (Éditions de Fallois, 1996) and *Histoire de Vichy* (Éditions de Fallois, 2004).
2.   Henri Frenay (1905-1988), the founder of the first Movement of Resistance, which would become Combat.
3.   Marc Bloch, professor of the history of the Middle Ages at the Sorbonne. He took refuge at Montpellier. He was one of the heads of the Free Marksmen. He was shot by the Germans.
4.   Former head of the General Staff of Marshal Foch; commander-in-chief from May to June 1940; high commissioner in North Africa, 1940-1941.
5.   The French air forces on November 10, 1942 contained, for example, 118 Dewoitine 520s more than in 1940; in all, 414 were available. The Luftwaffe and the Italian air would seize in November 1942 717 flyable planes. Cr. D'Abzac-Epezy, *L'armée de l'air de Vichy* (S. Hist. Armée Air, 1997).
6.   A. L. Funk, *Hidden Ally* (Greenwood Press, 1992).
7.   Source: Brault Report, in G. Lévy, "La Résistance armée," *Revue historique des armies*, 1969, 4.
8.   *La guerre en Provence* (Presse Universitaire de Lyon, 1998).
9.   Organization of the Army's Resistance, created after the occupation of the southern zone in November 1942.
10.   *Histoire de la Résistance*.
11.   F-G Dreyfus, *Le patriotisme des Français sous l'Occupation* (Éditions de Paris, 2000, published under the auspices of the Club Témoin).
12.   On the Resistance in Alsace and Moselle, please see our *Histoire de la Résistance*, pp. 351-364.

Bibliography

In addition to the two works cited above, *Histoire de la Résistance* and *Le patriotisme des Français sous l'Occupation*, this study is based on:

H. R. Kedward, *À la recherche du marquis*, Le Cerf, 1999, and the regional or departmental monographs of:

R. Bouladou, *La Résistance dans l'Hérault*, Montpellier, 1991.

A. L. Funk, *Les Alliés et la Résistance*, Aix-en-Provence, 2001; in English, *Hidden Ally*, Greenwood Press, 1992.

P. Gaujac, *La Guerre en Provence*, P. U. de Lyon, 1999.

P. Martin, *La Résistance dans la Drôme*, thesis, Paris IV.

J. Quellien, *Opinions et comportements politiques dans le Calvados sous l'occupation allemande*, dissertation, Caen, 1997.

From Resistances to the Resistance

Christine Levisse-Touzé

Introduction

I prefer the terms "resistances" in the plural and "diversity of activities and behaviors" to the phrase "nebula of devotion" (the literal translation of the original French title of this volume. Trans.), which has a negative connotation because of its vagueness and which causes a certain confusion in the reader or hearer.

On the other hand, I fully adhere to the definition of "resistance" given by Jean-Pierre Azéma and François Bédarida, as "clandestine activity conducted in the name of liberty, the nation, and the dignity of the human person, by volunteers who organize themselves to struggle against the domination (and most often the occupation) of their country by a Nazi, or fascist regime, or its satellite or ally."[1] It includes, therefore, in addition to armed resistance (guerillas, underground sabotage, networks of escape and evasion and of information), the most well known form, also civil resistance, that is, political and ideological resistance by means of propaganda (the diffusion of tracts and of newspapers) and, finally, humanitarian resistance, aiding the victims of persecution and of repression.

This is what emerges, moreover, from the historical works of the past few years, informed by colloquia that provided essential contributions: *Mémoire et histoire: la Résistance*, under the direction of Jean-Marie Guillon and Pierre Laborie,[2] *La France et les Français, enjeux stratégiques et environnement social*, a publication directed by Jacqueline Sainclivier and Christian Boujeard,[3] *Villes, centres et logiques de décision*, organized by Henri Rousso and the Institute

---

Christine Levisse-Touzé is director of the Jean Moulin Museum and the Leclerc Memorial. She is author of several books, including *L'Afrique du Nord dans la guerre, 1939-1945* and *Paris 1944*.

of Contemporary History,[4] and finally, *La Résistance et les Européens du Sud*, organized by Jean-Marie Guillon and Robert Mencherini.[5] These works suffice to show that, contrary to a still deeply rooted current view, the archives concerning the Resistance are abundant. It's enough to consult the seventy-two AJ holdings established by historian Henri Michel right after World War II, or those of the Central Bureau of Information and of Action at the Archives of France, to get an idea of their extent and richness. And does one still have to recall the great interest of the archives of the national gendarmerie, and those of the prefecture of police, for studying in their least details the actions and reactions of the French?

The diversity of actions and behaviors establishes the context of my contribution, as I will take care, following the injunction of Jean-Pierre Azéma, to avoid all "Gallo-centrism."[6] The Resistance must be placed in the context of the war: the attitude of the enemy, Allied operations and the diversity of their interventions. The work of American historians, who are well represented in this colloquium, has shown the role of the British services, the Intelligence Service (IS), the Special Operation Executive (SOE) (with its own service, Action, which sent agents and furnished assistance to the undergrounds), and, finally the American Office of Strategic Service (OSS). Their activity will intensify with the preparations for the allied landings in France.

On another plane, the example of the Drôme analyzed by Patrick Martin shows very well the social dimension of the Resistance and its patriotic motives. It joins in this regard the previously cited works.

One of the singularities of the French Resistance is connected with the evolution of the war and to the fact that there were two "resisting France's," fighting France (Free France and the interior Resistance beginning in July 1942) and the Giraudist Resistance, which appeared in Algeria as a fallout of the Torch operation of November 8, 1942. The other singularity is very important: the Resistance was able to find the path of unification.

Resistances

The motives of those who chose Resistance are many. Christian Pineau, however, cuts cleanly to the core: "In fact there was only one reason, one true reason, that sums up all the others: we will not tolerate them [the occupiers]." Lucie Aubrac explains her engagement: "In this extraordinary debacle, I immediately, and violently, reacted because I did not like it...that someone invaded my country." Daniel Cordier, nineteen years old, a student: "At the moment when Pétain announced the necessity of ceasing the fight, I considered [him to be] a traitor and, two, that it was null and void. If we really stopped fighting, we would not be able to resume it." Leo Hamon, a member of the Parisian Committee of Liberation and of Those of the Resistance: "It was not acceptable that France be defeated. It was not acceptable that our struggle against the Nazi system would stop." François de Menthon, a Christian Democrat who founded with Pierre-Henri Teitgen the movement Liberty, stated in the first clandestine issue of a newspaper published in the southern zone the meaning of his commitment: "Nothing is lost. The war can still be won. We refuse to acknowledge ourselves defeated. Even more, we refuse to help Germany defeat us."[7] These men and women chose to enter into the Resistance out of patriotism and because of ideological motives, the defense of the Republic and the anti-fascist struggle, finally, to fight against the German Nazi occupier. Sometimes they reacted against Marshal Petain's speech of June 17 announcing the Armistice, sometimes they reacted to the "appeal" of General de Gaulle on the 18th of June.

Many individual acts, soon followed by collective initiatives, characterized the beginnings of these resistances.

The examples are numerous. At Mt. Velay, less than two hours after having heard Petain's speech, General Cochet, commander of the air forces of the Fifth army, gave his men instructions to resist. At Chartres on June 17, Jean Moulin, prefect of Eure-et-Lore, with all of his strength and will opposed the Germans of the Eighth infantry division. Summoned to sign a document falsely accusing the Senegalese troops of the French army of the massacre of civilians, he refused. After the obligatory cigarette and fearing that he would succumb to torture, he tried to commit suicide by slitting his throat. Discovered at dawn covered with blood, he was taken to the hospital. He resumed his responsibilities even before he regained his health. Others thought to counteract propaganda. On the June 17, Edmond Michelet and his comrades of "the Circle" of social groups of Brive printed and circulated two tracts among the inhabitants. Before the war he had worked to help Spanish refugees and anti-Nazi Germans.

In July General Delestraint, saying good-bye to his soldiers, encouraged them to reject every "thought of the beaten dog or the slave" and concluded: "Confidence, again confidence, always confidence."[8]

Acts of sabatoge on electrical and telephone cables in the occupied zone (Royan, Nantes, Épinal...) were very early; their authors, subjected to the expedited justice of German military tribunals, were shot. This was the case with Étienne Achavanne, executed on July 6, 1940, for having cut on June 20 telephone cables in Rouen. Or that of Émile Masson and Lucien Brusque, who were shot at Saint-Valéry (in the Somme) November 12.[9] These are only a few examples.

The clandestine tracts, newspapers, or sheets were one of the principal means of those who wanted to alert public opinion and display their opposition to the Vichy government and to the occupiers. Among them were *Conseil à l'occupé* (in June 1940) and Jean Texcier's *Notre Combat* (September 1940).

In the autumn of 1940 the first clandestine newspapers appeared: *Pantagruel* of Raymond Deiss, *L'Avant Garde*, the organ of the Federation of Communist Youth, *L'Université Libre*, under the auspices of known academic and literary personalities—Frédéric Joliot-Curie, Paul Langevin, Jacques Solomon, and Jacques Decour—and *L'Homme Libre*, created by Jean Lebas, the mayor of Roubaix, former Socialist minister of Work and Employment.

Officers of the army of the Armistice, or those in retirement, who did not accept the defeat entered into the Resistance. They were more numerous than is regularly said. A recent study by General Delmas shows that of the "35,000 officers in 1939, 12,000 became prisoners"; and the remaining 23,000 divided themselves between 12,000 outside of the capital and 11,000 in the metropole (of them, 4,200 were in the army of the Armistice, 2,000 in the civilian bodies, and 4,800 took an Armistice leave of absence).

After November 1942, of these 11,000, 1,000 reached retirement age, 1,500 escaped by Spain for North Africa, 4,000 served in the Resistance, and the rest of the 4,500 abstained from all action.[10] Among these resisting officers, one of the most well known is Captain Henri Frenay who, with the assistance of Maurice Chevance-Bertin, former lieutenant in the colonial infantry, and Berthie Albrecht, created the Movement of National Liberation in the summer of 1940. At the beginning of 1941, knowing that the command would never give the order to reprise fighting, he took a leave of absence from the army.[11]

In September 1940 at Lyon the underground group Liberty came into being, thanks to the initiative of Pierre-Henri Teitgen, a professor of law, and François de Menthon, an economist. They were assigned, respectively, to the universities of Montpellier and Lyon. They associated with themselves Edmond Michelet at Brive, Charles d'Aragon in the Tarn, and René Courtin in the Hérault.

At Clermont-Ferrand, a small group, the Last Column, was established, thanks to Jean Cavaillès, a philosopher at the University of Strasbourg, another professor, Lucie Aubrac, and her husband, Raymond, Georges Zephara, a banker who belonged to the international league against anti-Semitism, and Emmanuel d'Astier de la Vigerie, a journalist. Also at Lyon, around Antoine Avinin, a former militant of the Young Republic, along with Jean-Pierre Levy, the group France-Liberty was formed. These groups became, respectively, Combat (which absorbed Liberty), Southern Liberation, and Free Marksman.

In September 1941, at Paris, thanks to the initiative of Raymond Burgard, a teacher at the Lycée Buffon, together with members of the Parisian section (15th arrondissement) of the Young Republic, the Valmy group came into existence. Some of its slogans were spread through London radio transmissions: "One enemy, the invader." "Hitler's vacuum cleaner reduces the country to less than nothing."[12] The first issue of *Valmy* appeared in January 1941.

The Resistance touched all social-professional milieus. Thus, Christian Pineau and Robert Lacoste, both active prewar syndicalists, decided to enter into the path of union resistance with the "Manifesto of the Twelve," which appeared November 15, 1940, a little after the dissolution by the government of Vichy of the principal workers' and employers' unions. The objective was to resist the directives of Vichy. Progressively put in place were the principal "channels" that would lead to the birth of Northern Liberation.

All regions were involved. The diversity of actions was very great. The first year of the Occupation was marked by a striking action in the North, organized by the Communist Party. This was the strike of the miners of the North and of Pas-de-Calais in May 1941, to fight against the increase in the pace of production essentially destined for the occupier.

On May 1, workers demonstrated their opposition by decking the smokestacks of factories with flags; in its turn, the Special Organization sabotaged mining installations and mounted a first direct attack against a detachment of German soldiers at Lambersart. The strike lasted from May 26 to June 9. The wives of the miners—there were four thousand—massively supported their husbands by demonstrating on June 4 at Billy-Montigny, denouncing the degradation of living conditions and demanding bread and potatoes. Identical demonstrations (called "housewife demonstrations") took place in December 1940 in Marseilles. Three hundred and nineteen miners were arrested between May 27 and June 17. Many were shot or deported.

Assistance was spontaneously put in place even before the signing of the Armistice, to save soldiers cut off from their units. After the Armistice, channels of escape and evasion sought to facilitate the escape of prisoners and their transportation to England. Each region—and notably the coastal regions—facilitated departures for England, the population furnishing false papers and clothes. One could cite many examples. We will mention Paul Joly, a manufacturer of Roubaix, who established the Caviar channel, in connection with the Belgian network Zero, in order to help people cross the line of demarcation, then the frontier at the Pyrenees. These first chains of escape transformed themselves into groups or networks, such as the group of Colonel Hauet for whom Germaine Tillion worked, which then melded at the end of 1940 with the Museum of Man. The English started their own networks (e.g., Pat O'Leary). Networks also operated in Belgium, such as Zero and Comet.

Other forms of resistance were put in place whose major objective was the collection of information about the enemy, for the sake of the British. Churchill feared a German landing. At the request of the Intelligence Service, Passy, head of the information services of Free France, sent agents into France: Raymond Lagier, called "Bienvenue," Maurice Duclos, called "St. Jacques," Alexandre Bereniskoff, called "Corvisart." Escapees from France swelled this initial team: Pierre Fourcaud, Gilbert Renault, Colonel Rémy, and Honoré d'Estienne d'Orves, who formed the networks Brutus, Confraternity of Notre Dame, and Nemrod. They were volunteers to perform information-seeking missions in France for the sake of the English, concerning enemy arrangements, ports, and train movements as well as electrical centers. At Marseilles, the Committee of American Assistance under the leadership of Varian Fry worked from October 1940 until the end of 1941 to organize the exile of German or Austrian anti-Nazi nationals and save them from being "handed over" to the German commissions, which was stipulated in the terms of article 19 of the Franco-German Armistice.

The first patriotic demonstrations on November 11, 1940 (a demonstration of high school and college students in Paris) attest to a rejection [of the Occupation], and underscore that the French were not as "wait-and-see" as has been said. To be sure, the beginnings were modest, but there were people in the midst of the ambient resignation who displayed their non-conformism, convinced that one must fight the occupier. The beginnings were also difficult and it was not always easy to connect at first effort with London. In a recent book, *Un évadé de la France libre*,[13] Georges Broussine nicely emphasized the problems. The first contacts were not always easy and occurred most often in the midst of already established friendships or socio-professional relationships.

The daily reality of the resister was not so removed from that of the non-resister. In fact, that was the best way of avoiding being suspicious. Dominique Veillon has analyzed the daily life of the resister: "At the beginning, nothing distinguishes the life of a resister from that of a non-resister."[14] The resister works, struggles with the problems of food and drink, transportation, heating. The privileged places of contact are above all public places that preserve anonymity. Only a small group of men and women are totally clandestine.

Thus these few resisters knew on their own how to shake off the general resignation. They will serve as points of reference for those who wanted to commit themselves to action despite everything. The initial resisters, with their initial tests and their initial sacrifices, brought hope and the beginning of a response to the trauma of 1940.

From Resistances to the Resistance

Until the mission of Jean Moulin to London in October 1941, the movements of resistance suffered from a lack of means (money and arms) and from their separation.

As we saw previously, Jean Moulin, prefect of Eure-et-Loir, committed his first act of resistance against the Germans on June 17, 1940. After his recall by the Vichy government on November 2, 1940, he settled as a farmer at Saint-Andiol in his native Provence.[15] His Republican patriotism drove him to continue the struggle, to establish contacts, and to unite others of goodwill who themselves were resisting the occupier. His objective was to gain London.[16] Having procured for himself false papers and the necessary visas, he composed in mid-October in Lisbon a synthetic document entitled "Report on the activity, projects, and needs of the groups established in France for the liberation of the national territory." This text was transmitted to the Special Operation Executive (SOE) and to General de Gaulle.

Envisaging the future, Moulin set out these goals: "It would be mad and criminal not to use, in the event of allied action on the mainland, these troops prepared for the greatest sacrifices, today scattered and anarchic, but tomorrow able to constitute a coherent army of parachutists already in place, who know the terrain and have already chosen their adversary and determined their objective." He also defined a politico-military plan of action with the putting in place of a unitary military organization. And he described the evolution of the actions of the three principal movements of the southern zone: Liberty, Liberation, and Movement of National Liberation, indicating that their heads had held a first meeting at the end of July, then a second at the beginning of September at Marseille. That meeting had ended with an accord concerning the principles of the independence of clandestine newspapers and of consultation on the various actions (demonstrations, sabotage) to undertake.

At his first meeting with General de Gaulle on October 25, Moulin defended his report in the manner of the prefect he had been. There had been other missions before his, that of Pierre Forman and that of Yvon Morandat. Something akin to an electrical current passed between the two men. Moulin made the head of the Free French aware of the dawning of a popular and democratic resistance. Until then, de Gaulle had had only a few contacts with the interior Resistance, which had come to life without him. The orders of mission that de Gaulle gave (November 5 and December 24) underscore the importance that he attributed to the political and military action of Moulin, who became his representative in the southern zone. The subsequent instructions of October 22, 1942 and of February 21, 1943 only completed things.

Difficulties began upon Moulin's return (January 1-2, 1942). The process of coordination had progressed during his stay in London: Menthon's movement—Liberty of the French—had been absorbed by the Movement of National Liberation of Henri, which created Combat.

Nonetheless, the movements were solicitous of their independence and were hesitant about the idea of common action that Moulin proposed to them during a meeting in March. He had to convince recalcitrant men, non-conformist and rebellious, attached to their autonomy and convinced of London's ignorance of their aspirations and those they represented. One must understand the independent and proud character of these men who had decided to enter the path of life-and-death adventure. Jean Moulin intended to rally each and all around the personality of the head of Free France in order to present one France in the struggle. The superior interests of France presided over this intention. He therefore had to make the interior Resistance recognize General de Gaulle. But the heads of the movements were hesitant with regard to this general, reputed to be Maurassian, and whose positions vis-à-vis democracy they did not know; they did not want him to "confiscate" their resistance. De Gaulle took away all ambiguity in a speech delivered at Albert Hall November 15, 1941.

In April 1942, the mission to London of Christian Pineau, one of the founders of Northern Liberation, was to obtain a promise concerning democracy from the head of Free France; this was an indispensable precondition for the unification of the Resistance. Pineau reports the "Declaration to the Movements" that the Resistance expected from General de Gaulle:

We desire
    That everything belonging to the French Nation would return into its possession.
    That the French people be its own master.
    That all of our interior liberties would be returned to us.
    That everything that detracts from the rights, interests, or the honor of the Nation
        would be punished and abolished.
    That the secular ideal of Liberty-Equality-Fraternity would be put into practice.
    That this war would have as its consequence an organization of the world establishing the solidarity and mutual assistance of nations.
    That once the enemy is chased from the country, all men and women of it would elect
        a National Assembly that would sovereignly decide the future of the country.

Before achieving such agreement, Rex—Moulin's pseudonym—had to overcome differences: the concern for independence on the part of the heads of the movements, problems raised by the creation of the secret Army and the nomination of its head. Frenay opposed it, because he wanted to impose his conception of a revolutionary army and he contested the separation of political and military action because it was difficult to realize, the same group of men being the foundation of both the political and military components of the Resistance.

The evolution of events assisted Moulin's activity. During the course of this year, 1942, anti-vichyism became general. The financial support that Rex could provide strengthened his position as the representative of General de Gaulle. At the end of August General Delestraint, formerly of the tanks, agreed to put in operation the secret Army. And, finally, under Moulin's influence there was the creation of central services—the Service of Aerial and Maritime Operations (SOAM), the Bureau of Information and the Press (BIP), the General Committee of Studies, the central organ for reflection that reemployed the groups of study already existing in Liberation and Liberty, and the Infiltration of Public Administration (NAP)— which allowed for the "structuring" of the Resistance.

The importance of the Resistance can be measured by the transformation that General de Gaulle effected of the Free French, turning them into Fighting France in July 1942, which aimed to integrate regular troops, the Free French forces, formed outside the national territory, and the movements of Resistance in the interior.

On October 22, 1942, de Gaulle extended the mission of Moulin. "You will have to assume the leadership of a coordinating Committee within which will be represented the three resistance movements.... On the other hand, you will continue as the representative of the national Committee in the occupied zone, making all the political contacts you can." De Gaulle, the head of Fighting France, encouraged the small organizations to affiliate with the larger movements in order to form more quickly a coherent force, a decisive consideration in the view of the Anglo-Americans.

The putting aside of General de Gaulle by the Allies during the landings in Morocco and in Algeria on November 8, 1942, and the political imbroglio that followed with the choice of Admiral Darlan as a provisional expedient, then the designation of General Giraud by the Americans as high commissioner, military and civilian commander-in-chief for North Africa and French West Africa, seriously called into question the legitimacy of the head of Fighting France. Giraud claimed that the Army of Africa (he claimed 300,000 men) would better represent France in the fight, with the weight of the AFN and the AOF, than General de Gaulle with his fewer Free French forces (50,000) and the colonies. "Giraudism" moreover had a certain impact: Giraud was the potential head of the organization of resistance of the Army. De Gaulle found himself in competition with Giraud for the direction of the French forces and territories in the war.

These decisive events encouraged the acceleration of the process of unification of the Resistance. Moulin's ability to negotiate allowed the "unblocking" of the situation. The interior Resistance became a card of legitimation for General de Gaulle; the political parties gave him their democratic approval, a major support to convince President Roosevelt of the importance of the Fighting French.

On January 26, 1943, a decisive step was taken with the creation of the United Movements of Resistance (MUR), the organ for the unity of command of the three movements of the southern zone. Parallel to it, the idea had progressively matured of creating a sort of clandestine parliament, by reintroducing political parties. The initial idea of creating a national assemblage was Christian Pineau's. Initially opposed, Moulin ended up agreeing, judging that the creation of a federative and representative organ otherwise would form outside the Resistance. While negotiations were underway with Giraud, de Gaulle had to have himself recognized by all the interior Resistance, in order to present himself to the Allies as the sole representative of France at war. General de Gaulle gave the order to Rex on February 21, 1943 to integrate the parties into the Council of the Resistance. Some have criticized de Gaulle, as well as Moulin, for having reintroduced parties. In the context of the period, though, it was unavoidable and normal, taking into account the role of the Communists (the importance of the FTP and the National Front) and of the Socialists (the Committee of Socialist Action) in the Resistance.

Getting things to work—Jean Moulin's job—was difficult because he encountered the hostility of the heads of the resistance movements to the introduction of parties and unions within the Council of the Resistance. The political parties of the Third Republic had been accused of being responsible for the defeat of 1940. The traumatization of France is important to keep in mind. A grave crisis of identity and of national conscience had occurred. All the heads of the movements, including Jean Moulin, were dubious. The principal movements were not composed of political men or of representatives of the traditional political forces but of individuals who represented for the most part "non-conformists." The resisters considered the old parties dead or moribund in the face of the birth of the new solidarities of the Resistance.

Pierre Brossolette, with the assistance of Passy, the head of the BCRA, was at the origin of the missions to organize a coordinating Committee for the northern zone equivalent to that of the southern zone. This body was created at the beginning of March 1943. Returning from London at the end of March where, with General Delestrait's assistance he had negotiated Allied assistance for the undergrounds, which were assuming a growing importance, Moulin brought new instruction from General de Gaulle. De Gaulle had named him the general delegate for the whole of France and had charged him with the task of creating the Council of the Resistance.

The general delegate authoritatively imposed unity: "We are at war, we must have a head and that head is de Gaulle." For Jean Moulin, the breakdown of unity would weaken France in the fighting. He reproached Brossolette for not having taken to heart the orders concerning the creation of the Council of the Resistance and for having given too much importance to the Civilian and Military Organization (OCM) in the northern zone, while leaving important groups out of the coordinating Committee, such as Resistance and Defense of France, whose newspaper was the most widely circulated in the northern zone. Moulin aimed to integrate the civilian movements.[17]

Moulin also had to overcome multiply difficulties. The Giraudist currents supported by the Americans remained powerful. Frenay, finding the cooperation of the Fighting French[18] insufficient, attempted, without alerting Moulin, negotiations in Switzerland with the American secret services in order to obtain means.

The political submission of Frenay to de Gaulle did not arrive as a matter of course. Combat failed to comply with instructions according to which the principal newspapers of the Resistance were to say, "One head, de Gaulle, one struggle for liberation," and instead had some editions say, "One fight for the country."[19]

Moulin met with the clandestine movements of the northern zone: Defense of France, Lorraine, Resistance, the Voice of the North, Rabelais. All were not going to join the Council of the Resistance. Not wanting to compromise the fragile equilibrium realized in the spring of 1943, Moulin ratified the choice of Passy and Brossolette: Defense of France therefore remained outside the Council of the Resistance. Moulin thus limited himself to preserving the eight large movements. He counseled the smaller ones to fuse with one of the larger ones, following the example of Resistance, which had done so with Those of the Resistance....

Moulin adopted the principle that the members who joined the Council of the Resistance ought to be invested with the confidence of the movements. At that time, their disaggregation as autonomous forces was already in motion and many of the former militants began looking again toward the parties.

One must emphasize the strong representation of Christian Democrats in the Resistance, for example, the movement Liberty, and among the bodies developed by Moulin, the General Committee of Studies with René Courtin and Alexandre Parodi, or the Bureau of Information and of the Press with Georges Bidault.

The stakes of this coming-together were important and bore upon the realization of unity in wartime, including the necessary understanding between de Gaulle and Giraud. The creation of the Council of the Resistance (CNR) was essential for this.

In order to overcome reticence, Moulin succeeded in imposing "political tendencies." On May 27, at the inaugural meeting of the CNR presided over by Moulin, sixteen formations were represented: eight Resistance movements (the three belonging to the MUR, Combat, Free Marksman, Southern Liberation, and five for the northern zone, OCM, Northern Liberation, Those of the Resistance, Those of the Liberation, and the National Front); six tendencies: Communists, Socialists, radicals, Christian Democrats associated with the parliamentary Right represented by the Democratic Alliance and the Republican Federation, and two syndicates, the CGT and the CFTC.[20] The motion read by Georges Bidault required that "the government...would be entrusted with General de Gaulle who was the soul of the Resistance from the darkest days, who from June 18, 1940 had not ceased preparing, in full lucidity and independence, the rebirth of the destroyed country, as well as shattered Republican liberties." It was requested that Giraud would be subordinated to him as military head.

It was less this meeting—which did have consequences in Algeria because it was not known about until much later—than the preliminary negotiations that brought to Giraud's attention the importance of the interior Resistance. When General Catroux announced to him on May 16 the creation of the Council of the Resistance, Giraud had already taken stock and decided to have General de Gaulle come to Algeria. The national Council of the Resistance was a unique organization in Europe.

Conclusion

The creation of the CNR assumed a considerable importance because it united all the forces of the interior Resistance. It brought the

support of the France fighting in the interior behind General de Gaulle
and opened the way to the formation in Algeria of a single organization to represent the nation. The creation of the French Committee
of National Liberation on June 3, 1943, under the dual authority of
Giraud and de Gaulle, was the prelude to the creation of a true government in which de Gaulle brought in the heads of the Resistance,
d'Astier de la Vigerie and Frenay (at the price of the progressive
eviction of Giraud), to the creation in November of the consultative
Assembly, and the reorganization of the French army in view of the
Allied landings and the reconquest of the national territory. From
Algeria, the organization of the public authorities of the Liberation
was in place.

Whatever were the difficulties that followed the arrest of Jean
Moulin and especially the emancipation of the resistance movements,
unity was not fundamentally called into question. It was essential to
the Liberation.

Jean Moulin's action had been decisive in settling General de
Gaulle's legitimacy in the Resistance and in unifying it. He also made
his contribution to the moral, political, and democratic reconstruction of the country. Thanks to Jean Moulin, the resistances became
the Resistance. His role was central, as André Malraux emphasized
when Moulin's ashes were transferred to the Pantheon on December
19, 1964: "Jean Moulin has no need of stolen glory: It was not he
who created Combat, Liberation, Free Marksman; it was Frenay,
d'Astier, Jean-Pierre Levy. It was not he who created the numerous
movements in the northern zone whose names the historians will
recollect. It was not he who made the regiments, but it was he who
made the army. He was the Carnot of the Resistance."

Notes

1.   Jean-Pierre Azéma and François Bédarida, "L'historicisation de la Résistance,"
      Esprit, n. 198, Paris, 1994, pp. 22-23.
2.   Toulouse, Privat, 1995.
3.   Presses universitaires de Rennes, 1995.
4.   Cachan, 1995.
5.   Acts published under their direction by L'Harmattan, 1999.
6.   Under the direction of Jean-Pierre Azéma and François Bédarida, *La France des
      années noires*, t. 2, *De l'"Occupation à la Libération*, Seuil, 1993, p. 241.
7.   Cited by C. Levisse-Touzé in the expository catalogue, *1940, l'année de tous les
      destines* (Paris-Musées, 2000).
8.   Germaine Willard and Roger Bourderon, *1940, de la Défaite à la Résistance*
      (Messidor-Éditions sociales, 1990), p. 102.

9.   C. Levisse-Touzé, op. cit., pp. 109-111. The Museum of the Order of Liberation presents many announcements of executions.

10.   The text of Jean Delmas appeared in *Officier et historien, etudes, articles, cours* (under the direction of Olivier Forcade, Pierre Lesouef, and C. Levisse-Touzé) (Economica, 2001).

11.   *Henri Frenay de la Résistance à l'Europe*, colloquium organized by the Ministry of Defense, Paris, National Assembly, October 19, 1995.

12.   Christine Levisse-Touzé, *1940, l'année de tous les destins*, op. cit., p. 111.

13.   Tallandier, 2001.

14.   Dominique Veillon, *Vivre et survivre en France 1939-1947* (Histoire, Payot, 1995), pp. 250ff.

15.   Saint-Andiol (Mouth of the Rhône), cradle of the Moulin family.

16.   For the missions of Jean Moulin, this study principally draws from the National Archives, the work of Daniel Cordier, *Jean Moulin, la République des catacombs* (Gallimard, 1999), and from the work published under the direction of Jean-Pierre Azéma and François Bédarida, *La France des années biures*. v. 2, *De l'Occupation à la Libération* (Seuil, 1999), and the chapter "Des resistances à la Résistance," p. 241ff., a study published under the direction of Jean-Pierre Azéma, acts of the 1999 colloquium, *Jean Moulin face à l'histoire* (Flammarion, 2000).

17.   Olivier Wieviorka, *Une certaine idée de la Résistance, Défense de la France, 1940-1949* (Seuil, 1995), p. 218ff.

18.   Free France became Fighting France at the end of July 1942, in order to accommodate the interior Resistance component.

19.   Archives of France, F1a 3728, *Rex* Dossier, report of May 7.

20.   Composition of the CNR: president, Jean Moulin; heads of Movements: OCM: Simon, CDLL: Coquoin, CDLR: Lecompte-Boinet, Northern Liberation: Laurent, National Front: Villon, Combat: Claude Bourdet, Southern Liberation: Pascal Copeau, Free Marksman: Eugène Claudius Petit. As for political tendencies: Communists: Mercier, Socialists: Le Troquer, Radicals: Rucart, Christian Democrats: Bidault, Democratic Alliance: Laniel, Republican Federation: Debù-Bridel. Organized unions: CGT: Saillant, CFTC: Tessier.

To Rehabilitate the Resistance

Maurice Delarue

My aim is to provide a defense, and to make a plea, for the French of the "dark years."

Why?

Because their detractors are legion.

The latter have always existed. In France, self-denigration is a national sport, but this masochism is today a luxury that we no longer can afford. After the trials of the world wars from which we emerged utterly drained, France was carried into a world economic, techno-logical, and demographic maelstrom for which nature provided her very few supports. Her only chance is to learn how to exploit them. But that still requires that she desires to do this, that she desires to be herself, that she desires to exist, and first of all that she rejects the caricature of herself that some present to her as her portrait: that of a puny people in times of trial, a people of cowards, of the craven, of racists, and of collaborators.

My sole ambition is to recall unquestionable evidence that politi-cally correct discourse today obscures.

First piece of evidence: Who voluntarily took up arms against Hitlerian Germany? Who deliberately declared war against it with-out having been attacked? Ask that question.

Confusing the capacity and efficacy of resistance with the politi-cal will to resist, people will say: America, Russia, Poland.... So many untruths. Only Great Britain with its "dominions" and France, on September 3, 1939, had the temerity to claim to block the route of the Wehrmacht, to respond to the German aggression in Poland. Afterwards, some distant countries declared war on Germany, for the most part a symbolic deed. Moreover, it is not to forget what we owe the British, who ten months later found themselves in the same

Maurice Delarue is a former journalist for *Le Monde*.

situation as us, that we emphasize that from September 1939 to the German offensive of May 10, 1940, France was alone on the front lines, with the support of about ten Allied divisions.

Another forgotten piece of evidence: France found herself in this tragic isolation, on the edge of an abyss, twenty years—just a generation—after having emerged victorious but bled white from the War of 1914, in which one Frenchman in twenty-nine died. Now, as soon as peace was restored she saw her great allies fail in their responsibilities—not without sometimes imposing their views on the war's aftermath—and ignoring the resurgence of dangers. Soviet Russia, which in 1917 had defected from the war, offered its hand to Hitler in August 1939, at a crucial moment; the United States refused to ratify peace treaties and the sketch of collective security that it had inspired, and retired into isolationism; Great Britain practiced *appeasement*, appeasement!—people thought they were dreaming, but the nightmare was real—with Nazi Germany until the destruction of Czechoslovakia, six months before the general conflagration.

That in these conditions the French in 1939 didn't have the requisite morale, how can one be surprised? But does that mean that they therefore refused to fight? 92,000 French soldiers died during the battle of France, a number of the same order as that of those killed—72,000 per month—before Verdun. Without prolonging this odious comparison, recall that the United States lost less than 300,000 men on all the fronts of the Second World War, in which they were the great victors, while in the same conflict France lost 250,000 soldiers and 370,000 civilians. These are figures that do honor to the American war leaders. But for God's sake, please do not impute the defeat of 1940 to a French lack of the spirit of sacrifice.

A connected question: In 1940 was France, according to a current expression, "ripe for fascism"?

The answer of those who lived during that period will be a shrug of the shoulders, while those who didn't live then take it as a settled matter, because of the regnant conformism that, yes, France was ripe for fascism.

That at the beginning of the 1930s there were Frenchmen tempted by a muscular populism, born of indignation against the impotence of the Third Republic, is uncontestable. But after the disturbances of February 1934 violence came to a halt and the last electoral consultation before the Occupation revealed, on the contrary, no fascist defection. More than the result—57 percent of the vote was for the Popular Front whose anti-fascism—on which it did not have the monopoly—alone made for its unity—another number unquestionably expresses the French attachment to democracy, that of electoral participation: 85 percent, a record that is underlined by the American historian William Shirer and a number that every democracy today would love to find in the ballot boxes.

Neither the occupier nor the Vichy regime, moreover, judged the small fascist groups of the pre-war to be exploitable. Only Doriot's PPF survived the flood. The other pro-Nazi formations, Déat's RNP, Deloncle's MSR, were creations ex nihilo of the occupier and members barely emerged from this nothing. The MSR of Eugène Deloncle, who ended up by being assassinated by the Gestapo, recruited 1,385 members.

German direct recruiting had relatively more success and the truly "hardcore" entered the SS. The Legion of French volunteers against Bolshevism recruited 11,000 volunteers of whom 6,500 were enrolled and 2,300 actually fought the Soviet partisans. The tricolor Legion recruited by Vichy for the same cause was a fiasco and the African Phalange destined to fight the Allies in North Africa only recruited 650 men. The only collaborationist creation that was important, which included up to 15,000 men, was the militia, a redoubtable supplementary police, which progressively, and rather fraudulently, exploited the patriotism of former combatants.

What's left is what was called "Pétainism."

To assert that in 1940 there were forty million Pétainists is an unverifiable conjecture. Let us admit it, however, since in the chaos of June 1940 the political debate hardly offered a choice. In the emergency the Pétainist consensus imposed itself by default. Still, one must specify what was then signified by the term "Pétainist."

Even if some politicians who knew him had once uttered the slogan, "It's Pétain we need," the French of the 1940s didn't know with any precision the political ideas of the Marshal. The only Pétain who was known—and respected—by all, including the first resisters, was not exactly pro-German: It was the victor at Verdun. No one then imagined that he would soon personify "the new order," Montoire and collaboration, that he would impose the statute of the Jews, call Laval to the government in June 1940, sack him in December and then recall him with enhanced powers in March 1942, legitimate with his prestige the obligatory work service (STO) in Germany and the militia, and name as ministers avowed fascists such as Brinon, Philippe Henriot, and Déat.

On the other hand, to be sure, there weren't lacking in the administration and even in the heart of the Vichy government Frenchmen who, wherever they found themselves and because they found themselves there, did everything, under the worst conditions, to save what could be saved and to serve their country. But my intention is not to weigh the merits and demerits of Vichy; it is to consider the judgment of the French. Whatever one may think of the justification of the government of that time and of its raison d'être up until the total occupation of November 1942, this fact remains: the French never had the possibility of pronouncing on its policies. There, however, is a simple way of knowing what they thought of it. It is to listen to Marshal Pétain himself reproach them for having "a short memory" and, for example, the following: "Frenchmen, I have important and serious things to say to you. For the past several weeks, from several regions of France, I sense an unhealthy wind stirring. Anxiety is overtaking minds, doubt is taking control of souls. The authority of my government is questioned.... A long time will be necessary to defeat the resistance of all these adversaries of the new order, but we must at present shatter their efforts by decimating their heads" (speech of Marshal Pétain of August 12, 1941).

That is clear. We were not, however, on the eve of the landing. The Liberation was far away. Nazi German was at the zenith of its power. The Americans weren't even in the war. After the conquest by the Wehrmacht of practically all of continental Europe, Russia, invaded in its turn, fought, while retreating, on all fronts. It was August 12, 1941, but the Pétain consensus was in the process of dying.

We are here at the heart of a controversy that has lasted for sixty years: Was the France of Vichy the France of the French?

One of the most significant aspects of the new order was obviously the lot assigned to the Jews. No one can ignore or deny the persecutions to which the Jews were subject in occupied France and I would not be able—a full day would not suffice—to discuss Vichy policy towards them. Putting to one side an ignoble anti-Semitic propaganda (which wasn't the government's alone), the implicit policy of Vichy consisted in delivering foreign Jews to the Germans while relatively protecting French Jews. Raul Hilberg, the author of the most complete work of history on the subject (*La destruction des Juifs d'Europe*, Gallimard, 1996), wrote concerning France: "Foreign Jews were abandoned to their fate and people tried to protect the national Jews. This strategy succeeded to a certain extent. By giving up the protection of a fraction, one saved the greater part of the whole." Three-quarters of the Jews of France escaped deportation, in contrast to a half in Belgium and a quarter in the Netherlands; but only 2,500 survived of the 75,000 Jews who were deported, the majority of whom were of foreign origin.

That being said, what was the personal conduct of the French? Of course, during its history France, like all of Europe, was not exempt from anti-Semitic racism, notably in the immediate prewar period. But there were few countries where the condemnation of a Jew because he was a Jew provoked an historical scandal that was not put to rest a century later (i.e. the Dreyfus Affair).

Despite anti-Semitic campaigns and movements, France nonetheless was considered to be welcoming to Jews *by Jews* who sought refuge here, especially in the 1920s, until the crisis of 1929. When the United States closed its borders in 1924, France became the largest country of immigration. I extract these statistics from the *Histoire des Juifs de France* by Esther Benbassa (Le Seuil, 1997). From 1906 to 1939, between 175,000 to 200,000 Jews came to live in France, 15 percent of the total immigration, and—I continue to quote Miss Benbassa—Paris became "one of the most important Jewish centers in the world."

Did anti-Semitism express itself in daily life? Here I cite one the most moving testimonies written during the distress of the dark years, in 1941: "I very much loved France and I served her with all my strength. I never experienced that my identity as a Jew put the least obstacle in the way of these sentiments." This Jew was the historian Marc Bloch, who was shot by the Germans on June 16, 1944.

All those who lived during the Occupation knew specific cases of racist denunciation or of racist cowardice, but in the gigantic chaos of the time what was the importance of these behaviors? Weren't they the exceptions? A final judgment on the entirety of a country at a time when all public liberty was banished demands the eye and the distance of the historian.

To my knowledge the best study of the subject, the most complete, the most precise, is a large work whose author, Israeli academician Asher Cohen, is little suspected of partiality: *Persécutions et sauvetages* (Éditions du Cerf, 1993). He writes the following: "We do not find recorded any sign of an active and extensive anti-Semitism in the [French] population, we find no proof that the anti-Jewish policy was actively or passively supported."

Asher Cohen indicates that the police, on the contrary, displayed a "sympathetic reaction towards arrested Jews." "The exclusively anti-Jewish newspapers didn't sell. The relative failure of the Final Solution [in France]"—writes Asher Cohen—resulted "from the weakness of the fascism and the racism of the 1930s." "It wasn't anti-Semitism," he comments, "it was racism" that "revolted consciences." This is a judgment corroborated by another specialist of the Occupation, he also little suspected of indulgence towards anti-Semitism, Serge Klarsfeld. In the weekly *Marianne* of September 8, 1997, he wrote: "There were very few letters of denunciation [in France]. The Germans had to raise the level of reward offered in an unsuccessful attempt to raise the number: The reward was raised from 100 to 5,000 francs for each denounced Jew."

A study by Antoine Lefebure of the censorship of the mail, *Conversations secrètes sous l'Occupation* (Plon, 1994), also attests that denunciations were nowhere widespread and that in the privacy of familial correspondence the French did not hesitate to display their hostility toward the government. Let those who have saved the letters of that period reread them and, apart from for the given exception, they will be surprised by the free tone. I myself did so recently and I found in the first letter I received after the arrival of the Germans, from a friend who was completely ignorant of my sentiments, words of this sort: "One will plunge me into a Pétrain before saluting me with a 'Heil Pétain!'"[1] These sarcasms and jokes were circulating currency. In the occupied zone, once the shock of the first days had passed, disrespect and derision were the attitudes most commonly inspired by Vichy.

Despite what is said today, subversive sentiments were soon expressed. People should recall that on November 11, 1940, less than five months after the entrance of the Wehrmacht into Paris, high school and college students demonstrated by the hundreds at different parts of the capital and above all at the Étoile and on the Champs-Élysées. There were people hurt and Vichy, after four days, acknowledged 123 arrests and closed the University of Paris until the end of the trimester.

A small but significant fact: movie cinemas had to keep theaters lit during the showing of current events—German, of course—so that spectators couldn't use the darkness to express themselves. Others will speak to you here from firsthand knowledge of behavior of an entirely different sort and import, especially the assistance given to Allied pilots shot down over France. I, however, would like to cite a sentence of Georges Broussine, the founder of the Bourgogne network, a channel of escape and evasion for 300 pilots, in a book of souvenirs that he had the humility to wait until today to publish: "Without the active or passive complicity of the immense majority of the French, no serious action against the occupier would have been possible."

It seems to me necessary, though, to insist on this point: It is almost impossible to bring upon the conduct of our compatriots during these "dark years" a categorical summary judgment. On one hand, the conditions of life have changed much from that time to ours, and above all, on the other, because public opinion then could not freely express itself. The press and the radio were controlled and censored. British and Swiss radio, the only sources of credible information, was not heard everywhere. The French could not have the same judgments, depending upon whether they lived in Paris or Alsace, or in Brest, Lille, Lyon, Nice, or Vichy.

During the first two years, to live in the occupied, or the free, zone, was to live in two different countries: in France, despite what one thought of its regime, or in internal exile in a hostile country. It was completely normal to feel oneself better protected in the southern zone. What I can attest to is that in Brittany where I lived, where one was bathed in the waves of the BBC, Vichy was very quickly judged severely and massively. Justly or unjustly, the State authorities and the occupying authorities were pretty much put in the same category by those they administrated. Witnesses and historians will speak to you about other regions. I do not doubt that they will speak, as Professor John Sweets does in his book on Clermont-Ferrand, about "surprising discoveries calling into question received wisdom."

It is not true that during the World War of 1939-45 the mass of the French people were craven, racist, and informers. It is not true that in 1940, either before or after, the French made themselves Hitler's accomplices. They were defeated in 1940 because they had incompetent leaders in a battle in which they alone, by themselves, held the first line. Many other armies were also defeated on all fronts before—more than two years after the battle of France—Hitler's advances were arrested by the combined assaults of a heterogeneous, but powerful, coalition of the greatest world powers.

What divided the French was not their objective. With certain very rare exceptions, all, including pacifists and anti-militarists, loathed Hitler and Nazism. What divided the French were means, tactics, and, even more, motives. Some were motivated by anti-German atavism and the memories of the Great War; others by the rejection of dictatorship and of racism, by attachment to liberty, democracy, and to the Republic; others were fascinated by Communism in the Soviet manner; others thought that Marshal Pétain and his avatars—Weygand, Darlan, and even perhaps Laval—were using indispensable masks and provisional expedients in order for France to regain her strength; others, finally, who weren't the most numerous at the beginning but became so, were moved by pure and simple patriotism inspired by General de Gaulle.

It was on this heterogeneous terrain that what de Gaulle from June 18, 1940 had called the "Resistance" spontaneously took root and secretly developed in the disorder and the sadness; it was the word taken up by Marshal Pétain but in order to condemn it, in his speech of August 12, 1941.

The Resistance is improbable if one imagines it as a rational, hierarchical organization, dictated from above. Rather than saying "Resistance" with a capital R, it would be more exact to say that there were resisters, some engaged very early, others a little, or much, later, many others who were simply occasionally available, who chose not to belong formally to this or that group but who took risks at a time when, given the presence of the Gestapo, the SS, or the militia, there were no small risks.

I do not believe that I can put the nature of the Resistance better than the historian Henri Michel:

> Viewed from above, the clandestine activity resembled the scattered, fevered work of an anthill. Each insect was occupied with its own miniscule task, none seeming to be concerned with that of the others, their paths crossing and intermixing, their efforts appearing to be vain, disordered. And yet a finality, an invisible order, commanded this hill: the solidarity and permanence of the collectivity.

A "national" anthill, "teeming with millions of obscure, humble deeds, sometimes—alas—unavailing, always dangerous…it brought together, if I can put it this way, ordinary men, the run-of-the-mill, who as such didn't leave the gray zone; some, however, were raised above themselves, they became heroes without having sought to do so. But all shared the vocation, the call, to be heroes" (*La Guerre de l'ombre*, Grasset).

Note

1.   The first part of the phrase is a play on words, which roughly translates as "into a nasty mess."

The Resistance in Clermont-Ferrand and in Auvergne[1]

John F. Sweets

First of all, I would like to thank you for having invited me to join you, and I must ask you to excuse me for not always perfectly expressing myself in your lovely language. I hope that my "Tennessee French" does not hurt your ears too much.

More than thirty years ago when I began my research into the Resistance in France, I had in mind an image of Épinal, of an organized, strictly hierarchical resistance, commanded from London, then from Algeria, by an all-powerful de Gaulle who was followed without debate by an entire nation of patriots in France. Like the majority of Épinal's images, in looking more closely one understands quickly that the reality was more complex, more nuanced. My first book, entitled *La politique de la Résistance en France*, was a study of the United Movements of the Resistance (MUR), which was the largest and the most important (non-Communist) resistance movement in France; above all it was the movement that provided Resistance in the southern half of the country. As the title of my book indicated, my attention was directed to the summits of the Resistance. The questions it asked were those concerning the political relations among the three movements (Combat, Liberation, and Free Marksman) that fused at the end of 1942-the beginning of 1943, to become the United Movements of the Resistance; their relations with the political parties, especially with the Socialists and the Communists; and their relations with General de Gaulle and other leaders of

John F. Sweets is professor of history at the University of Kansas. He has taught as a visiting professor at University College, Dublin, and at the Université de Franche-Comte in Besançon. He has published numerous articles about France during the Second World War and two books, *The Politics of Resistance in France* and *Choices in Vichy France* (published in France as *Clermont-Ferrand à l'heure allemande*).

the organizations of the Free French. This approach to the history of the Resistance gave me the privilege, and the great honor, of meeting in the 1960s and 1970s the great heads of the French Resistance. Whether Lucie and Raymond Aubrac, Pascal Copeau, Alban Vistel, Georges Bidault, and many others spoke to me about their own experiences in the Resistance, or whether they shared with me documentation that they had kept during these dark years, these willing contributions very much enriched my work and my knowledge of the Resistance.

Nonetheless, this first effort remained limited in the sense that it was a study "from on high," which above all treated the higher echelons, the national heads of the movements, the members of the National Council of the Resistance, and it generally stopped at the level of the regional heads of the MUR, without getting very close to the grassroots militants, nor to the complicitous networks they found in the general population. I received wise counsel from Pascal Copeau, who told me in a 1970 interview that one should pay attention not to be deceived concerning the total validity of the "organigrams" of the Resistance, which were prepared by the high command or the staffs outside the country. To be sure, one can trace the lines of contact between the leaders in London or Algeria and the resistance organizations in the interior, and the latter are divided into different sectors and services (propaganda, information, sabotage, networks of escape and evasion, and so on) that one can represent in a schematic fashion. But despite the desire of the higher leaders and the Gaullist agents sent into France from the outside who wanted the activities to be partitioned, kept separate, the men and the women of the groups or units did a little bit of everything in the resistance movements. In addition, these were volunteers, not conscripts. Therefore one didn't give them orders "from above" without an explanation, without having to convince them of the necessity of one action rather than another. One must seek at the local level the living reality of the Resistance, Copeau told me.[2]

For my next project, therefore, I turned my attention toward Clermont-Ferrand and Auvergne.[3] There, I in fact found that the Resistance was much more complicated, more fragmented, more variable with the passage of time and of circumstances than I had realized. And more important in the context of the principal theme of our colloquium today, I understood that in order to describe accurately the climate, or to retrace the history, of France under the German occupation, one must reformulate the definition of the Resistance. A definition limited to the active members of organized groups has the advantage of greater precision, but such a limitation inhibits a just appreciation of the full phenomenon of resistance. A larger definition of the term "resistance," encompassing the concept of active opposition to the Vichy regime and to the Germans, is certainly more difficult to manage. But it is also conforms more to the complex reality of the Resistance in France.

In order to render more specific the methodological and interpretive problems posed by this definition, let's begin with a widely circulated statistic that speaks of perhaps 400,000 people, about "2% of the adult population of France,"[4] who belonged to the organized movements of the Resistance. If one begins with this estimate, there would have had to be about 13,000 resisters in the entirety of Auvergne and 5,000 in Puy-de-Dôme. Even though an exact breakdown of their numbers is impossible, different sources allow one to fix appropriate totals, both maximum and minimum, to the participants in the formations of the organized resistance. After the liberation, 35,000 people took cards as members of the Movement of the Liberation (the successor to the MUR) and 6,500 as members of the National Front. These figures include numerous sympathizers and those who joined at the last hour, and were certainly inflated with respect to active partisans. A police report considered the number of clandestine adherents to the MUR/MLN in Puy-de-Dôme to be more probably 15,000; and according to the testimony of Alphonse Rozier, a total of 5,000 active members for the National Front in Auvergne was closer to the truth than the 10,000 advanced by certain members of the organization.[5]

If the maximal estimation indicated by these figures is the accurate one, 17 percent of the adult population of Puy-de-Dôme would have actively participated in the Resistance, while according to the lowest one, perhaps 7 percent. If one only takes into account the men engaged in the regular formations of the FFI at the Liberation (around 16,000 for the region, 10,000 for Puy-de-Dôme), the total remains higher than the 2 percent proposed by several historians but it is closer to this estimate. One can then conclude that the number slightly superior to the mean of FFI in Auvergne simply expresses the fact (which is generally admitted) that because of its mountainous character, the region was one of the most active centers of the Resistance. But to stop at this conclusion would be to accept a much too narrow definition of the Resistance. The FFI were not the only participants in the Resistance, neither in Auvergne nor elsewhere.

One must not forget, for example, that at least 543 people not contained in the foregoing figures were shot "for acts of resistance" in Auvergne; that more than 1,000 people were arrested by the Germans in Puy-de-Dôme in 1943 and 1944; and that at least 1,171 (non-Jewish) inhabitants of Puy-de-Dôme were deported to concentration camps in Germany or in Central Europe, as well as hundreds of others suspected of resisting in the three other administrative districts of the region.[6] Add several hundred people arrested by the French police because they were suspected of Communist propaganda or of activities said to be "anti-national." And recall the massive opposition to the STO, from which several thousand Auvergnans escaped by means of acts of direct disobedience. Then the total number of individuals actively implicated in opposition to Vichy and to the German occupation, even if it remains a minority, becomes an important minority. Moreover, we have spoken until now only of individuals who, after long and detailed researches, were able to be identified and individually counted. What can one say of the men and women who, if they didn't figure among the members of a formation, nor on the lists of the deported, the shot, or the imprisoned, nonetheless rendered important services to the Resistance? Should one forget the doctors of Puy-de-Dôme who, without being members of movements of resistance, sabotaged the STO operation and the attempts at recruitment for railway guards by signing certificates of physical incapacity for individuals of whom the police complained that they continued "to ply normally their trade"?[7] How many country priests showed their courage by sheltering resisters sought by the French and German authorities, or what to say of those men and women who procured work, nourishment, or shelter for the members of the underground or to the individuals who were constrained to depend upon the locals?[8]

On November 11, 1943, the anniversary of the Armistice of 1918, in response to tracts signed by the CGT, the MUR, the National Front, and the Socialist Party, hundreds of workers of Ollier, Bergougnan, Michelin, and other large factories of Clermont-Ferrand stopped work from between ten to fifteen minutes to eleven hours in a symbolic deed of protest; the thirty shop girls of Prisunic showed their solidarity, silently crossing their arms.[9] Several months before, when Marcel Michelin was arrested by the Germans, the 7,000 employees of the manufacturer were ready to go on strike: the leadership persuaded them that such an action risked doing more harm to their "patron."[10]

Beyond these incidents—and one could give other examples—is it possible to quantify the passive resistance displayed by increased absenteeism at workplaces? In particular, in the last months of the Occupation the rates of absence were at least 20 percent higher than normal in the factories and mines of Puy-de-Dôme.[11] Even if the loud explosions attracted greater attention to the sabotages of the Resistance, some resisters judged another form of sabotage to be very important, silent but more subtle, which consisted, for example, in poorly calibrating the high precision elements of airplane engines that they were responsible for manufacturing.

It should be noted that concerning the most important industrial sites of Clermont-Ferrand, the Michelin factories, the enterprise remained very much under its production capacity and succeeded in dissimulating a rather large part of that fact from the German inspectors.

One could continue to draw up an impressive list of people responsible for deeds who were not connected with any organized resistance: the fifteen-year-old adolescent who on his own initiative burned the dossiers of hundreds of young people requisitioned for the STO;[12] the employees of a mayoralty who, assigned to collect and melt down metal statues, saved them from destruction by creating delays and falsifying documents;[13] the heads and the personnel of the central hospital of Clermont-Ferrand, suspected by the police of "tacit connivance" with resisters and with political prisoners who seemed to escape with remarkable frequency when they were being treated;[14] or numerous agents of the PTTs, to whom the heads of the Resistance rendered a special homage for the courage and regularity with which they alerted them about troop movements or police operations of the German or French forces.[15] A complete list would be at least as impressive as that of the most spectacular sabotages and surprise attacks of the formations of the organized Resistance.

What was the cumulative impact of these individual acts of opposition to the Vichy regime and to the German occupation? It is impossible to measure the misfires and stoppages they inflicted on the functioning of the German war machine. Who really knows how many airplane engines failed in flight or how many tanks broke down on the Eastern front because of acts of sabotage committed in the factories of Clermont-Ferrand? What we do know, on the other hand, is that the factories of Clermont-Ferrand working for Germany were always late and behind in their production, despite the surveillance of German inspectors.[16] No one is going to claim that the hundreds of thousands of French men and women who listened to the BBC or who read and passed along to their friends clandestine newspapers were heroes, no more than were those who participated in symbolic strikes of short duration or who blended anonymously in the crowds that assembled on the squares to demonstrate on May 1 or July 14. And yet, and yet, all that was illegal in Vichy France, and these were conscious choices, not entirely without risk.

Eugène Martres estimates that one inhabitant of six of Cantal, one way or another, had ties with the Resistance, either as a sympathizer or as an active member. According to him there could be ten sympathizers for each resister.[17] It has been impossible for me to arrive at a satisfactory estimate for Puy-de-Dôme, even though the number of resisters and their level of activity was certainly higher than in Cantal. After more than fifteen years of research into this question, I am convinced that (except for a very individualized census in the next life) we will never have perfectly convincing statistics for the French Resistance. It therefore is necessary to go beyond the finally insoluble problem of a precise individual breakdown in order to attempt to assess the general atmosphere, the climate within which the Resistance operated during the years of German occupation. I would like to direct your attention to a particular element of those years that were so difficult, so painful, in the history of your country. This element is the silence.

What did the silence during the German occupation signify? And how has the silence become a subject of controversy among historians? In the 1970s my compatriot Robert Paxton wrote a famous and influential book in which he maintained that the absence of active opposition, the silence, and the wait-and-see attitude of the French population had rendered it complicit with the collaboration of the Vichy regime. I quote him: "Even the recalcitrants, because they didn't put into doubt the legitimacy of the regime and didn't pose an active opposition, came to increase, without wanting to do so, the wave of partisans. All these groups, from the tepid to the fervent, are 'collaborators' in the functional meaning of the term, because they created that large current of opinion which, first of all recognizing the legitimacy of the regime, went next to participating more actively in it."[18] Even if I share most historians' admiration for Paxton's work as a complete study of the Vichy government, having closely studied the realities of the region of Clermont-Ferrand concerning what the attitude of the French population was during the Occupation, I come up with a different image than that of my American colleague. As I said in my study:

> The majority of the population had abandoned, if not all, at least the greatest part of its sympathy for the Vichy regime a long time before what was to be the most unpopular act of the regime, the introduction of obligatory work service. Therefore, to insist on a wait-and-see attitude on the part of most French, their apparent indifference, their apathy, their resignation under the Vichy regime, and to describe them as "collaborators in a functional sense," given the emotional and ideological charge of the word "collaboration," does not acknowledge the necessary distinction between opinions and actions and perverts the common meaning of the term. Shouldn't indifference and apathy rather be interpreted as opposition to, rather than support of, a regime, especially a regime that committed itself on all fronts to stirring up enthusiasm for its program and its leaders? If one had to choose a formulation to describe the sentiments of the majority of the French under Vichy, functional resisters would be more worthwhile than functional collaborators.[19]

This idea of "functional resisters" can be illustrated with reference to the many senses of the word "silence" during the Occupation. Everyone knows the famous clandestine novel of Jean Bruller (Vercors), *The Silence of the Sea*, in which an old man and his niece refused to speak to a French-loving German officer who had commandeered their house. As the American editor of the English version of this text, which came out in the United States in 1944, wrote, the novel expresses the opinion of millions of French who believe that "these men are going to disappear under the weight of our disdain and we will not even give ourselves the trouble of rejoicing when they are dead."[20] At first glance silence is a difficult subject to treat for an historian. It is in fact "nothing" or the absence of something, the absence of sound or speech or noise. Therefore, one could think that it would leave very few traces in the documentation of a period. But by following these traces, I submit to you that one very quickly finds indubitable signs of this unrecognized Resistance for which one is seeking in this colloquium.

Let us limit ourselves to a few instructive examples. It is obvious that for the press of the period, silence was demanded by the Vichy government concerning anything that could trouble the Germans. The archives of the newspaper *La Montagne* of Clermont-Ferrand are filled with directives from the Secretary General of Information demanding that Alexandre Varenne, the independent editor of the newspaper, should conform to the will of the government (which he most often refused to do). The censor's hand ensured that at the time of the total stopping of the publication of *La Montagne* in August 1943, Varenne and his newspaper possessed the record in the southern zone for the greatest number of suspensions due to violations of the instructions of the censor. At this time everyone knew that nothing was printed in the newspapers without the okay of the Germans and of Vichy, and in the face of the imposed silence on subjects that interested them they sought their news in clandestine newspapers or on the BBC.[21]

Noting the sympathetic and compassionate reactions on the part of the public to the first deportations of foreign Jews, the regional superintendent of police of Clermont-Ferrand indicated to the commander of the units of the reserve mobile guard charged with a mission of rounding up Jews in Puy-de-Dôme, that his troops should leave Clermont-Ferrand for Bourboule under the cover of night and thus "avoid showing themselves to the public";[22] the men should not be informed of their destination and objective until their arrival at the place of rounding-up. That is to say, *silence before the public* in order to avoid the latter's disapproval, *silence before their men*, in order to avoid them giving the alert to those who were sought: silences that say much about the attitudes of the population.

During the years of the Occupation one is struck by the importance that the word "silence" plays in the reports of the police and gendarmes charged with the surveillance of the population. Month after month they bitterly complained about the silence of their fellow citizens who refused to answer questions posed concerning the location of refractors, the activities of the underground, Jews hiding in the area, et cetera. Seeing that in 1943 the Jews they were looking for in the villages of Puy-de-Dôme had almost always departed when the police arrived at the appointed place, certain police officers complained of being general laughing stocks.

Eventually, a police inspector at Clermont-Ferrand was deported by the Germans for aiding the Jews. The undergrounds and the Jews hidden in the country could survive only on one condition: "that they be protected by the population that supplies them, shelters them, doesn't reveal them, and warns them about every threat."[23] In Auvergne they found this so-necessary welcome and they found it in that unrecognized resistance about which we are speaking.

The Auvergne police frequently complained about "a veritable conspiracy of silence"[24] in which most Auvergnans were accomplices. It would be inexact to claim that their silence transformed them into active resisters, but this lack of cooperation with the agents of the Vichy government was the reflection of the popular opposition to the regime, and not a form of support. It is not doubtful that the regime's leadership interpreted the situation in this way. The repeated complaints of leaders at all levels, regretting that the population had not understood that it was supposed to support the government's efforts, that the people refused to make good choices, etc., show clearly that the majority of the French had less and less sympathy for the Vichy regime as the months passed.

To conclude, one could consider the phenomenon from another point of view, that of the militiamen, the most ardent of the collaborators. In November 1943 German observers noted: "Whoever joins the militia exposes himself to the worse vexations and runs the greatest dangers,"[25] and at Clermont-Ferrand it was noted that "officials show themselves equally very hostile to the French militia, whom they consider as a surveillance element of the public services in general."[26] Therefore it was not surprising that a month before the Liberation the head of the militia of Auvergne, Jean Achon, asked for a rather particular silence on the part of the public of Clermont. It appears that on the occasion of a funeral procession the population had shouted insults at the militiamen killed in a battle with resisters. Achon proclaimed that many of the militia made the sacrifice of their life for these French who insulted them, and he concluded bitterly: "At least they could have better respected their memory!"[27]

In my view, it is obvious that the memory that ought to be respected and honored today is the memory of that unrecognized resistance, which made possible first the survival, then eventually at the Liberation of France the triumph, of that Resistance. I thank you for your kind attention.

Notes

1.   Auvergne, one of the twenty-two regions of France, is located in the central/south-central part of the country; it contains four administrative districts (trans. note).
2.   Interview, Pascal Copeau, January 23, 1970.
3.   John F. Sweets, *Choices in Vichy France* (New York, Oxford University Press, 1986).
4.   Gordon Wright, "Reflections on the French Resistance" *Political Science Quarterly* LXXVII: 3 (September 1962), pp. 336-49.
5.   For an evaluation of the numerical importance of the groups of resistance, see M06336, January 25, 1945 (Departmental Archives of Puy-de-Dôme: ADPdD). Information note, General Information, on the integration of former FFI in the

regular army; see also several documents on the pay of the FFI in M09457, ADPdD, and the monthly reports of the prefects and the commissioners of the Republic after the Liberation; letter of Alphonse Rozier to the author, January 14, 1981. *L'Annuaire statistique regional retrospectif* (Clermont-Ferrand, INSEE, 1964) provides the basic statistical data on the population that I used in my calculations of the percentages of participants in the Resistance.

6.   One will find the lists of names and of figures of the executions, the arrests, and the deportations in M06643, M07244, M09361, and R91807-08, ADPdD; see also Daniel Martin, "Statistique de la déportation," department of PdD, from June 1940 to August 1944.

7.   M04869, ADPdD, December 22, 1943, the prefect of PdD. His letter asserts: "In certain towns, the number of those exempted for reasons of health exceeds a third of the people eligible for requisition."

8.   In M05538-40, ADPdD, documents concerning the people who sheltered deserters from the STO; M09642, Report, prefect of PdD, February 5, 1945, treats the activity of the clergy.

9.   Relevant documents in M07161, ADPdD.

10.   M06357, ADPdD, July 6, 1943, General Information, n. 4284.

11.   M05787, ADPdD, statistics and comments concerning production; RW 24/275, April 11, 1944, Rüstungskommando C1-Fd, "Darstellung der rüstungswirtschaftlichen Entwicklung in der Zeit vom 1.1 bis 31.3.1944," Militärarchiv, Fribourg.

12.   Letter of Rozier to the author, January 14, 1981.

13.   Numerous documents in M05794, ADPdD.

14.   M06357, ADPdD, December 27, 1943, n. 38007, central commissioner to the superintendent of the police.

15.   M05843, ADPdD, Commandant Martial notes that the PTT merited a "very laudatory" citation.

16.   Figures for the production of the Rüstungskommando of Cl-Fd in the series RW 24, Militärarchiv, Fribourg.

17.   Martres, *Le Cantal de 1939 à 1945*, dissertation (University of Clermont-Ferrand, 1974), pp. 301-302.

18.   Robert O.Paxton, *La France de Vichy 1940-1944* (Paris, Le Seuil, 1973), p. 225.

19.   John F. Sweets, *Choices in Vichy France*, pp. 168-169.

20.   Vercors, *The Silence of the Sea* (New York, Macmillan Co., 1944), p. vii.

21.   Sweets, *Choices in Vichy France*, pp. 146-149.

22.   M07153, ADPdD, March 25, 1943, regional superintendent of the police to the commander of the GMR of Auvergne.

23.   As François Marcot wrote about the *refractaires* of the STO in his dissertation, *Résistance et population (1940-1944)* (University of France-Comté, 1994), p. 80.

24.   M06357, ADPdD, June 5, 1943, Generation Information n. 2711, jacket for June, July, August 1943; and M07191, August 25, 1943, monthly report, central commissioner to the delegate-prefect.

25.   "Sonderbericht Nr. 9: betr. Die franzosiche Miliz," p. 8 (Captured German Documents, National Archives, Washington, D. C.).

26.   M07191, ADPdD, February 23, 1943, central commissary, Cl-Fd, to the delegate prefect.

27.   M06133, ADPdD, Achon to M. Pierre Prier, regional delegate for information, July 21, 1944.

American Contacts with the Resistance

Arthur L. Funk

When we discuss the role of these "unrecognized resistances" during the Second World War, we may wonder if among the actions done by Americans to aid the Resistance some have remained unknown to the French public. Everybody knows, of course, the American soldiers, the GIs, and such famous names as those of Eisenhower and George Patton, but many are those whose deeds are now forgotten, despite many books and specialized articles, as well as commemorative memorials.

Let us take the example of an event that took place right in the heart of Paris, in the fifth arrondissement. A plaque on a wall of Rue Tournefort reminds us that "Here in 1943 and 1944 Mrs. Andrée Goubillon hid and gave shelter to forty-two French paratroopers, members of the Resistance network Sussex plan, under the command of Colonel Malcolm Henderson, for the liberation of France."

The Sussex Plan

The Sussex operation indeed is not very well known and yet today there exists an association of its former members and a museum dedicated to its missions. Americans, British, and French took part in this operation, which had for its goal information gathering. Some of its members are the well-known Rémy (Colonel Roulier) on the French side, Colonel Henderson for the British, and Major Havilland and Captain Alden for the Americans. Before August 1944, the

Arthur L. Funk, professor emeritus at the University of Florida's Department of History, is a specialist on French-American relations during the Second World War. He served in the U.S. Navy during the war, and has been cultural attaché in Syria, Madras (India), and Madagascar. He has published a "trilogy" of books on U.S.-French wartime relations, and over thirty articles. As a vice-president of the International Committee on the Second World War, he has participated in many conferences in Europe, including two in Moscow. Most recently a French edition of his *Hidden Ally* (on the landings in Southern France) has appeared.

Sussex operation had successfully dropped into France eighty-four secret agents who relayed seven hundred and twelve coded messages before the Allied landing. The current president of the association is Louis Guyaumard (alias Monestier), a former resister in Brittany.[1]

The Sussex plan was put in place in 1944, but few people know that the Americans, even though they had officially recognized the Pétain government, secretly worked with the Second Bureau against the Germans. At the beginning, the military attaché was the liaison officer between the two parties but, after the attack on Pearl Harbor and the entry of the United States into the war, a special envoy of the American secret services, Thomas Cassidy, a former World War I pilot, was in charge of that mission. Cassidy had been a member of the La Fayette squadron with Captain Louis Baril who in 1942 became head of a section of the Second Bureau. Frank Knox, the secretary of the Navy, sent Cassidy to Vichy when he discovered that the two men were friends. Thanks to Baril and other anti-German members of the Second Bureau such as Colonels Rivet, Ronin, Villeneuve, and Paillole, Cassidy was able to use the diplomatic bag to send information to the Allied headquarters. He also set up connections with André Girard who was the head of the CARTE network. This particular network was hampered in its work for reasons that would take too long to explain here. My main concern is to emphasize the following point: despite the fact that the United States had official relations with Vichy and not Free France, it did establish contacts with the Resistance even before entering the war. After the general occupation of France following the landings in North Africa, Cassidy was detained in Germany and this initial contact was broken. On the other hand, Henri Frenay, Pierre Guillain de Benouville, and Henri Frager maintained their relations with Americans in Berne and, later on, in Algeria.[2]

The OSS (Office of Strategic Services)

In June 1942, General William Donovan, who had been the Co-ordinator of War Information (CWI), became the head of the Office of Strategic Services (OSS), and initiated a rapid increase in American clandestine operations.

In 1990, Fabrizio Calvi produced an excellent study of the OSS, *OSS: La guerre secrète en France*, one of very few books about this organization to be published in France. At the beginning, Calvi states that, "the details of the actions of the OSS in France are not in any history of the Resistance." The reason why used to be the lack of sources of information, but archives are now available. Calvi continues: "When we went to Washington to study these documents, we wanted above all to do justice to those clandestine networks so unjustly forgotten and to make our contribution to the history of the Liberation. We wanted to bring a radically different and fresh perspective to the study of these events, not to write a 'new history of the Resistance.'" This unprecedented point of view raised a whole new set of questions: What had been the contribution of each network to the liberation of France? What would have been the impact of the clandestine networks, had they been deprived of American help?[3]

To answer these questions and get a more accurate idea of the activities of the OSS during the war, we not only would have to make an in-depth study of Calvi's book, but also analyze more closely the archives of the OSS. Here, I will concentrate on a few important points, beginning with the situation in Algeria.

Donovan concentrated on North Africa as a result of having been forbidden by the British secret services to base himself in London. In addition, the United States was then supporting General Giraud and the OSS therefore worked at the beginning with the French intelligence services. After the Allied forces had landed in North Africa where Colonel Baril helped the American army, the OSS set up an office in Algeria and developed its networks.

Frederick Brown (alias Tommy) is generally recognized as the first American agent in France. However, his Anglo-Saxon-sounding name should not deceive us: in fact he was not American. He has been variously said to be Canadian, Ukranian, or even from Luxembourg. In 1938, he had opened a radio repair shop in Algeria and worked in that capacity for the French, the English, the Poles, and the Americans. Later on, he was introduced secretly into Corsica and then France, where he contributed to the creation and development of the networks that would convey information essential to the troops that landed in Normandy in 1944.[4]

The information gathered by the OSS networks in France (it sent over 8,000 secret reports) was declared "precious" by the planners of the landings in France. The OSS archives in Washington include an impressive array of messages sent by various groups such as

AKAK, UPUP, HOHO, HIHI, and ZUZU. In 1944, AKAK was send-
ing three suitcases of documents a week from Toulouse to Barcelona.
These documents contained descriptions, drawings, and maps of
German installations.[5]

Special Operations

Much more could be said about the information services, but that
would be at the expense of another, little known, aspect of the operations of the OSS, namely the guerilla warfare and sabotage its
members participated in with the French Resistance. From the beginning of the war, the British Special Operations Executive (SOE),
had developed methods—in an equally nebulous area whose details are little known in France—which allowed agents and supplies
to be shipped by plane. Several Americans played an important part in
this field even though only two of them are mentioned in documents.

The first one is Virginia Hall, an iron-willed, one-legged woman
who left her job at the American Embassy to work with the various
"circuits" of SOE. She worked in Lyons first, using the protective
cover of the activities of a journalist. Later on, she was assigned to
work in the Creuse, in Paris, and in the Haute-Loire region.

The second one is Denis Johnson, the radio operator of the Marksman network of the SOE. He was part of a three-man team that was
parachuted into the Ain area. The other two men were J. P. Rosenthal,
a Frenchman, and R. A. Heslop, an Englishman. In Heslop's absence, Johnson was in charge of providing all the necessary supplies for the network circuit. He became the liaison officer between
the regular forces and the FFI in August 1944 as the Allied forces
were closing in on Grenoble. In addition, he was one of the first
editors of *La voix du maquis*, a newsmagazine for the French underground of Ain and the Haut-Jura.[6]

Johnson was also a friend of Romain Petit's assistant, Henri
Girousse (alias Chabot). Girousse's southern group liberated
Meximieux and Pérouge with the help of American infantrymen in
1944.

At the time of the summit meeting of the Group of Seven in Lyons,
President Clinton, before an audience of a thousand people, reminded
them of this common fight to free Pérouge from the Nazi occupiers.
He took advantage of his visit to meet former members of the underground, in particularly Henri Girousse, who at the time was the presi-

dent of the Association of the Alumni of the Undergrounds of Ain and of the Haut Jura.[7]

The "Carpetbaggers"

Missions such as these depended directly on the pilots and the planes that carried men and supplies from England and North Africa. Transportation was assured by British planes based at the secret airfield of Tempsford and the American 492nd Bomb Group based at Harrington in Northhamptonshire. The code name for the USAAF operation was "Carpetbagger." Being an American historian, I deal mostly with the American activities but we must not forget that the British began their operations as early as 1940 and organized thousands of parachute drops before the Americans arrived on the scene. In 1943 American aviators were sent to Tempsford to be trained by RAF pilots. The 801st Bomb Group (later renamed 492nd) included sixty-nine B24s (Liberators), five A26 attack bombers (Invaders), seven Mosquitoes, and four unarmed C47s (Dakotas). The planes painted in black were adapted for low-altitude night flights.

The results of the Carpetbaggers, even though less important than the RAF, were nevertheless impressive. In a mere eight and a half month period (January-September 1944), they flew 2,300 missions: 1,650 of them were successful, and dropped 377 men, 19,184 containers, and over 10,249 packages of arms, ammunition, and equipment. Losses unfortunately were heavy: twenty-six Liberators crashed and 208 crewmembers lost their lives.

The first C47 (a Dakota) to land in occupied France made it on July 6, 1944, on the airstrip of Izernore in Ain. Its pilot was Clifford J. Heflin, the group commander. It was planned that the plane, heavily camouflaged, would remain on the ground until the following day. The crew and passengers were welcomed by the underground and by Denis Johnson, the American member of the SOE network who worked with Romain Petit. Upon his return to England Colonel Heflin declared: "I strongly recommend that every assistance be given to the troops of the underground, for I have never seen such courage anywhere." The Dakotas accomplished thirty-six "true" missions above France, the rest being classic liaison and transport flights. Between June 6 and September 18, 1944, the C47s (Dakotas) carried about forty-eight tons of materials, including jeeps, dropped seventy-six agents, and repatriated approximately 213 people.

In 1993 a memorial was dedicated on the clandestine airstrip of Izernore. And the day of September 5 was dedicated to the memory of Denis Johnson. The president of the Committee honored him in the following terms: "An American officer joined the ranks of the underground and rapidly became a great friend.... Up until his death in February 1993, this big-hearted American remained among us. We will mourn him forever, so great is his place in our hearts.... On September 5 he will truly be among us on two accounts.... For an impressive delegation from the 492nd, headed by Colonel Fish and Lieutenant Colonel J. W. Bradbury (he too a former "carpetbagger"), will join us at Izemore when we dedicate the memorial."

All these operations were part and parcel of the "secret constellations." Today there is still an important association of former carpetbaggers, whose French representative, Serge Blandin, lives in Lyons. (There are other representatives in Great Britain, Denmark, Belgium, the United States, and Norway.) The association is particularly interested in the French aspects of these missions: the agents, the dropped equipment, the search for shot down planes. Around fifteen monuments and plaques bear witness to the memory of these crews in France.[8]

Operational Groups

The OSS also included American commandos, called Operational Groups (OG). Normally, two officers headed each thirty-man unit. Twenty-one such OGs, i.e., over 500 soldiers, took part in the battle over France: one in Corsica, fourteen from Algeria were in the South and the North, one in Brittany, three in central France, and two in Burgandy. These commandos placed themselves under the command of the FFI leader in the department. They were more heavily armed than the members of the underground and thus were most welcome as they usefully reinforced the local military structure. Their contribution was "nebulous" and little known; I must observe, however, that the military historian, Colonel Paul Gaujac, speaks about them in his book, *Les forces spéciales de la Libération*, and gives a brief summary of their activity.[9]

The Jedburgh Operations

The OSS continued to work with the SOE and the BCRA and also participated in other relatively little known operations. One of these

was the Jedburgh program. The Jedburgh teams had three men: one
of them had to be French, the other two could be either French,
English, or American. They had radio contact with London or Algeria and acted as liaison agents between the FFI in the field and arms
and equipment providers. Out of the 278 soldiers who made up the
ninety-three teams that were dropped in France, eighty-three were
American.

CHLOROFORM, DANIEL, and GREGORY are examples. The
CHLOROFORM team (Jacques Martin, Jean Sassi, and the American Henri McIntosh) was dropped in the Drôme in 1944 and helped
the FFI liberate [the Belmont] Gap.

The DANIEL team included two Englishmen, K. J. Bennett and
R. Brierley, and one Frenchman, Captain Alfred de Schonen. They
were first dropped in Brittany. Then the team was renamed GREGORY.
It landed near Besançon on September 5, 1944 along with the
ETOILE mission. The two groups came near enemy positions on the
banks of the Doubs River but they fell victim to a German ambush
and four out of the nine men (including Captain de Schonen) were
wounded. Nevertheless, the group continued its activities and sent
messages to London up until mid-October.

Unfortunately, for lack of time I cannot speak more about the
Jedburgh teams. However, I want to say that the Jeds still get together under the presidency of Ambassador de Schonen. Many of
them are still alive and some have had remarkable careers. William
Colby went on to become the director of the CIA. On the French
side there are Philippe Ragueneau, Ambassador de Schonen, General Le Borgne, General Carbuccia, and General Aussaresses, among
others.[10]

Americans also played a part in other special missions and I want
to comment upon two of them: the MARCEL PROUST mission and
the SOE SACRISTAN network.

The MARCEL PROUST Mission

The PROUST mission also had as its purpose to send French and
American agents into France on an intelligence-gathering mission.
Colonel Waller Booth headed the team made of two Frenchmen,
Lieutenant André Carnut (real name, Guermantes) and Lieutenant
Charmand (real name, Marchadier), and two Americans, Captain
Mike Burke and Lieutenant Walter Kuzmuk, who had learned how

to speak Ukranian as a child. The group was dropped in Franche-Comté on September 10, 1944 and quickly established contact with the underground in the Confracourt forest, twenty kilometers from Vesoul.

It just so happened that two members of this underground, Simon Doillon and Claude Vougnon, were on friendly terms with a Ukranian contingent of 700 men who had escaped from the German yoke and joined the Confracourt underground. Kuzmuk could speak with these men: thus he became the liaison officer of the Ukranian battalion (known as BUK). This battalion was to be transferred to the Foreign Legion and participated in the battle of Belfort Gap.

The Booth team arrived not only at the time of the Ukranian episode but also at the time the first elements of the Seventh army (the 117th Cavalry) approached Vesoul. Booth met the Cavalry's commanding officer at Port-sur-Saône and the two men agreed that the MARCEL group and a contingent of the underground should join them and be used as skirmishers and scouts doing reconnaissance work for the forces.

Such a symbiotic relationship became useful during the long winter months of the battle in the Vosges. The courageous Simon Doillon was one of its casualties and the city of Vesoul cherishes his memory, considering him as belonging to the first rank of their "resisters." Vougnon, his companion in the fight, survived the war. Colonel Booth also left his imprint in Haute Saône. At his death in 1986 *L'Est républicain* wrote: "A very large, courageous, nice, strong-willed, and serene man. Praise will never be lacking to extol this native of Kentucky who recently passed away at the age of 82. He lived in Haute Saône for two months in 1944 and came back twice to revisit us."[11]

Ernest Floege and the Lomont Mountains

We should not forget the SACRISTAN group and its commander, Ernest Floege. Born in the United States of French parents, Floege returned to France as an adult. He participated in two missions in France. During the second one, he was in charge of the SOE SACRISTAN "circuit" east of Besançon. At his arrival in Franche-Comté in May 1944, Floege operated between the Doubs River and the Lomont mountains with the Montbéliard group, commanded by Captain Joly. At the time of Joly's death, Floege (known by the name

Captain Paul) took over and became for most of the partisans "the unchallenged commander of the network, the only one." After the Allied landing in southern France the Lomont group grew, to the point of counting over 3,000 members.

In anticipation of the Allied arrival, Floege and several FFI groups set up as many ambushes as they could and defended the Doubs' strategically vital bridges. General de Lattre underlined their contribution: "the most significant event of today's destabilizing efforts occurred at the far eastern end of the Lomont mountains where Linarès met an FFI group under the command of the American, Captain Paul. For three months this group, despite its isolation and several German attacks, successfully defended this steep plateau and the old fort that crowns it. This exploit—worthy of admiration—delivered to us an incomparable watch point over the Montbéliard plain and "the watchdog" of the Belfort Gap."[12]

Conclusion

Many are the individuals composing the "unrecognized resistances" who took an active part in the liberation of France without receiving the honors they merit. I hope to have made my contribution to their recognition.

Notes

1.   Fabrizio Calvi, *OSS: la guerre secète en France* (Paris, Hachette, 1990), pp. 283-291; Louis Guyomard, "Le plan SUSSEX," *Icare, Revue de l'aviation française, aviateurs et resistance*, 1994/1, 3; Douglas W. Alden, "Sussex and Proust: A Worm's Eye View of OSS," *French American Review*, 63, 1 (Spring 1991). SUSSEX is particularly close to my heart because Captain Alden is a former colleague (professor at the University of Virginia) and because he recently died.
2.   Calvi, op. cit., pp. 112-115; M.R.D. Foot, *SOE in France* (London, MHSO, 1996), pp. 204-208.
3.   Op. cit., pp. 15-16.
4.   Calvi, op. cit., pp. 55-60, 145-161 and passim.
5.   A. Cave Brown, ed., *The Secret War Report of the OSS* (New York, Berkley, 1976), pp. 480-489. See also A. L. Funk, "Intelligence and Operation ANVIL/DRAGOON," in the International Commission of Military History, Acta n. 13, Helsinki, 1991.
6.   Calvi, op. cit., on Hall, pp. 337-340, on Johnson, pp. 27-29, 37-40, 245-250, 454-467.
7.   Patrick Veyret, *Résistance armée dans l'Ain* (Châtillon-sur-Chalaronne, Taillandier, 1999), pp. 25, 37, 142-160.
8.   Calvi, op. cit., pp. 449-461, report of the DAKOTA operation, interview of November 24, 2000 at Lyon with Serge Blandin.

9.   Paul Gaujac, *Les forces spéciales de la Libération* (Paris, Histoire & Collections, 1999), p. 397 and passim; and my book, *Les Alliés et la Résistance* (2001), which describes OG actions in the South.

10. Arthur Brown, "Les Jedburgh: coup de maître ou une occasion manqué," *Guerres mondiales et conflits contemporains*, n. 174 (April 1994), pp. 127-144. Brown is also the author of *Jedburgh: A Short History*, available on the internet at: http:// freespace. virgin.net/authur.brown2/teams.htm. The reports of the Jedburgh teams and the OG's are found at the National Archives in Paris, 72 AJ 84 (7, 8, 11).

11. Calvi, op. cit., pp. 494-497; Georges Coudry, *Les camps soviétiques en France* (Paris, Albin Michel, 1997); Waller Booth, *Mission Marcel Proust* (Philadelphia, Dorrance, 1972); Michael Burke, *Outrageous Good Fortune* (Boston, Little Brown, 1984).

12. Ernest-Fred Floege, *Un petit bateau tout blanc*, published by the author; Colonel R. Dutriez, "Le maquis du Lomont," *Résistance FFI* (Bulletin de la Fédération des Amicales des FFI: du Doubs, Jura-Nord, Territorie de Belfort), n. 21, 1995, pp. 39-53; Henri Noguères, *Histoire de la Résistance en France*, v. 5 (Paris, Laffont, 1981), p. 745; Jean de Lattre de Tassigny, *Histoire de la première armée francaise* (Paris, Presses de la Cité, 1971), p. 156.

The Resistance in the Drôme[1]

Patrick Martin

As with a nebula, the contours of the "popular Resistance" are defined by a view of the whole. The historian is like an astronomer or a biologist: what he studies moves in time, when he observes it in detail he loses the vision of the whole, and vice versa; it is the constant back-and-forth between several levels of observation that allows him a complete knowledge of the system studied, in its dynamics and its interchanges.

It is in this context that this exposition of the civilian Resistance in the Drôme administrative district situates itself.

1940: Gestation and First Developments

On July 14, 1944, the departmental Committee for the liberation of the Drôme, in the first issue of its newspaper *The Resister of the Drôme*, made an appeal for the general mobilization of the men and women of the region: "We expect not only assistance, but we demand the full participation, without restriction, of our fellow citizens."

Some of these fellow citizens had already participated in the Resistance a long time, rendering it more than "assistance."

The first forms of civilian resistance in the Drôme were precocious. They corresponded to a patriotic state of mind tied to a certain courage, with a refusal to be subjected to the situation brought on by the war, which went beyond religious, philosophic, or political cleavages. These forms were individual as well as collective, and they did not integrate themselves (with rare exceptions) into a more general movement, even an embryonic one.

Thus, for example, on June 25, 1940, in the north of the Saint-Donat district, in her home taken over by the Germans, Mady Chan-

Patrick Martin is Agrégé of the University and Doctor of History at Paris IV-Sorbonne.

cel[2] did not accept the champagne that an officer offered her. The latter asked her, "You don't like champagne?" "Yes," she replied, "but I don't drink when my country is unhappy." The officer leaned forward and said, "I understand, Madame."[3]

In July, "the Protestant pastor Marc Boegnere protested against the commitment to deliver German political refugees to Germany."[4] In August, "Albert Triboulet,[5] teacher of Italian at the Romans'high school, was contacted by an attorney from Grenoble, a Mr. Hugues, to participate in a clandestine network of resisters."[6] September 11, "Raoul Pontet, a café owner in Romans, a militant Communist, was arrested for the flagrant crime of Communist propaganda and the possession of Communist tracts,"[7] "when he reproduced 'the appeal of July 10, 1940' of Thorez and Duclos."[8]

October 28, 1940 "certain inscriptions in chalk in favor of de Gaulle's movement were posted in different places, but the population paid no attention."[9] Others opposing the new regime encountered the same lack of interest. Around November 11, a group of high schoolers of Valence[10] published and circulated the first tract against collaboration: "Remember Clemenceau. Clemenceau said, 'To collaborate with the enemy, is to betray.'"

In his report of November 11, the prefect of the Drôme indicated "the apprehension of certain Catholic circles concerning the introduction in France of measures that in Germany gave rise to the protests of confessional milieus. But these worries are modest." He added "that mail surveillance reveals the bitterness of Protestant circles, as well as of the army of Salvation. Protestants [are] subject to Anglo-Saxon and Swiss influences, whose pastors are not from the localities."[11]

Some will be quickly informed of the reality of the Germany occupation by two early demonstrations that weren't of Drômian instigation. On November 20, 1940, "the Lorrainian refugees of Romans and Bourg-de-Péage organized a patriotic demonstration that local authorities attended."[12] Then on the 30th, "[a]n identical ceremony took place at Bourg-de-Péage. Songs and 'The Marseillaise' concluded this fine demonstration. The refrain of the 'Marche lorraine'—'You will not have Alsace and Lorraine...'—was repeated by everyone in attendance."

The prefect was not mistaken about the danger of such demonstrations, especially since refugees from Alsace and Lorraine took up residence in many Drômian towns. In his December 16, 1940 report he wrote: "An evolution favorable [to the policy of collaboration] was clearly perceivable after a few days, but one also must recognize that the expulsion of the Lorrainians had a disastrous effect. They arrived in the state of mind I described elsewhere, and they constitute everywhere as many propagandists, that it would be very dicey to want to reduce them to impotence in a short time."

In this report, he shows that the war will take place also on the propaganda front and the behavior of the population will depend on it. He describes the basic points of departure of this propaganda campaign, as far as the Drôme is concerned: the Drôme "has been for many years the prototype of the old Republican department. There still reigns here a certain mystique that the events of June haven't entirely dissipated." Therefore he knows that he has to convince the hesitant, who "form the immense majority and are found in all the milieus...they are at the mercy of the propaganda that events themselves will produce, as well as the propaganda that the authorities will know how to produce. It is to them [that he attempts] to address [himself] in every circumstance. [He tried] to recruit some lecturers or speakers who, as need be, could go out and make the right message heard where necessary. This recruitment, however, has proven to be very difficult. The Drôme does not appear to be a climate favorable to public enthusiasm." This difficulty in finding propagandists doesn't really concern the partisans of Vichy: "those of General de Gaulle are small in number, Communist action appears to have its point of origin in Isère, the SFIO milieu doesn't budge."[13]

1941: The Time of Latency

This propaganda front extended during the course of 1941. German propaganda only and always having a negative impact,[14] one can observe the clash between that of the Allies (which includes that of the French Resistance) and that of Vichy. The civilian Resistance will be both the performer and conduit of Allied propaganda. The aspects already seen in 1940 will be intensified.

At the beginning of the year tracts were distributed, papers and posters affixed to the walls of certain towns or cities, directed against the government or the organs of Vichy. At Die the gendarmes identified "an individual of the Jewish religion" responsible for these posting, whom they didn't manage to arrest, since he left the town. Individual actions of the civilian Resistance occurred throughout the duration of the war, including when they were very dangerous. August 20, 1944, when the deportees on the last railway convoy were passing through the district and had to change trains and walk from Loriol to Livron, "the sentinels asked a press gang heading toward the Drôme where the German baggage was.... Then an air alert occurred. The sentinels took shelter. Ten meters away was a peasant with his towing truck. Twelve deportees...escaped thanks to him and joined the underground."[15]

In February 1941 the Allied began the parachute drops of the "Mail from the Sky."[16] But the BBC was the most effective means of propaganda they possessed. It could be used to initiate actions of the civilian Resistance whose impact was certain; above all, it allowed for the increase of "conversational" propaganda. In March "the French section of the BBC took up for its own sake the instruction given by the Belgium section to its listeners on January 13, 1941, and asked its listeners to trace 'Vs' on all the walls, something easy to do, without great risks."[17] The gendarmes of the Drôme noted numerous "V" inscriptions from May until August, which forced them to be more vigilant in order to diminish the number. The gendarmerie found itself equally obliged to look for "the indiscreet auditors" of the propaganda that it had the duty of combating;[18] such listeners, men and women, who were caught risked imprisonment. In certain communes, a part of the population already constituted a majority in favor of the Resistance, which was strong enough not to be too worried. After two demonstrations on July 14 at Saillans, where people cried "Long live de Gaulle!" and at Bordeaux where French and British flags were placed at the top of the tower that dominated the city, the head of the gendarmerie of the Drôme reports that "the people in these small locales distrust the gendarmerie and distrust each other: no one wants to talk, to say what he really knows. And the inquiring gendarmes come up against a very great silence, even on the part of people who would be able to identify those who make trouble."[19] The inquiring gendarmes not only came up against a great silence among the people: at the time of the posting of fliers against the Legion in Saillans in February, the local gendarmerie had not completely revealed it.[20] At the beginning of January, a police commissioner had dissimulated a Gaullist demonstration he had witnessed.[21]

Everyone did not exhibit the same indulgence that year, and arrests occurred when the opponents of the Vichy government protested on the occasion of the first anniversary of the Legion, at the end of August. In October at Crest, Mrs. Rivoire, "former teacher who conducted anti-national Revolution activities and frequented people known for their antipathy to it defaced posters of Marshal Pétain."[22] On December 8 she "was squealed on and arrested and accused of derogating the dignity of the head of State; she was detained at Lyon until January 29, 1942."[23]

Popular resistance, resistance on the part of the people, thus was not without its risks; in such cases it diverted the attention of the gendarmes to a "secondary" sort of resistance, which one very soon notes is rooted in a part of the populace.

Individual actions turned toward listening to the BBC, toward graffiti, and hisses in theaters can easily avoid repression. But for the people whose civilian resistance activity went beyond simple protests, clandestinity imposed itself from 1941.[24] Take, for instance, Marguerite Soubeyran who, according to her own testimony, that summer sheltered at her school in Dieulefit "eight Jews coming from the school of Bourboule who belonged to the Rothschild foundation, which had been disbanded." It was also an obligation for the Resistance movements that implanted themselves in the Drôme during that year.

On December 20, 1941, the sub-prefect of Nyons concluded that, "as a whole the people don't show very much eagerness to accomplish the national Revolution.... Moreover, minds for several years have been oriented toward an ideal that is opposed to the current aspirations.... Little by little elements that are clearly hostile show themselves."[25]

Permit us to note here another form of resistance that seems rather rare: that tied to humor. We have only found one witness who mentions it, Jean Veyer, who refers to a "joke" heard in Die in November 1941.

1942-1943: Vichy Loses on All Fronts of Civil Society

During the course of 1942 the Vichy government definitively became unpopular.[26] It lost on the symbolic front.

That summer several statues were taken down for their metal. And Saillans made itself noticed again: On July 29 "the municipality of Saillans took down from its pedestal the bust of the Republic for it to be turned into non-ferrous metals. In the night of July 30-31, this statue was stolen by some unknowns.... An inquiry was opened.... No one would talk, the great majority of the population was very glad that the theft had taken place."[27]

It lost on the front of daily life. For example, on December 3, 1942, Law n. 1061 forbade "the sale, retention, the transportation, and the bearing of firearms of all kinds, including hunting weapons...Article 4: every holder of the arms or ammunition defined in Article 1 must deposit them, within a period of ten days dating from the publication of this decree, in places that will be designated in each district by order of the prefects.... Article 7: every infraction of the dispositions of Article 1 of the present decree will be punished with the penalty of solitary confinement. When the retained arms constitute a supply depot, the guilty will be taken to a special tribunal and punished with the death penalty."[28]

The arms depots of the CDM were handed over because of this law. But the general population was ignorant of the existence of the CDM; men were more touched by the interdiction of hunting weapons and they found ingenious means to hide them, some (self-centered individuals) knew better how to hide their rifle than to participate in the Resistance by hiding refugees.[29]

During the summer lack of supplies in the villages led to demonstrations of housewives in Romans in June, in Valence in July, which were not suppressed. Unfortunately, all our efforts to discover the organizers have been in vain.

More than the difficulties of daily supplies, it was two decisions by the Vichy government, the relief force[30] and the deportation of Jews, then the invasion of the southern zone by the Germans, that unleashed the collective reactions of the popular Resistance.

Organized by the different Resistance movements from all quarters, the demonstrations protesting against the relief force marked a *structured* engagement of a popular Resistance. The first strikes took place at Romans October 29, 1942, together with a demonstration. Other strikes took place in the same town[31] November 5.

There were no demonstrations against the deportation of the Jews, as there were against the relief force. These deportations (which began August 25, 1942) led the Vichy regime to lose ground, though, on the religious front. On September 8, "following a protestation of Mgr. Saliège at Toulouse and Romans, Jean Perriolat, the departmental director of the JOC, wrote in the militants' program: 'precision on the Jews. Gerlier letter'"[32] and on September 22 the Protestant church of France sent a message "to the faithful of the Reformed church of France, which was a vigorous protest against the measures striking the Jews. It was to be read in all parishes October 4, 1942. Pastor Eberhard read it at Dieulefit October 25."[33] The reactions of protest could be stifled, as in the region of Saint-Vallier where, on August 29, "four handwritten posters and five wall writings protesting against the arrest of the Jews were discovered by the gendarmerie and immediately ripped off or erased. This event prompted a serious inquiry...without its authors being able to be identified." Protection of the Jews dates from 1941, and the organization it required found popular support in the religious and political communities of the Drôme, which limited arrests and deportations,[34] thanks equally, until August 1943, to the Italian authorities.

After the Axis spread into the southern zone, this popular base welcomed and supported the undergrounds. For example, in the northeast of the district, in Grand-Serre, where the mayor and a part of the population will shelter some of Lieutenant Geyer-Thivollet's men. After remaining some weeks in various farms, they constituted the first Northern Drôme underground.

At the end of 1942, the prefect could not fail to observe that "the propaganda gatherings [in favor of the government] in the towns only attract a small number of true believers and have no effect on the masses."[35] One year later, the commander of the gendarmerie of the Drôme confirmed: "The general situation in the department has clearly gotten worse since last month. The state of mind of the population has become bad. Even though the situation with the different branches of the economy...has not noticeably evolved, and one can observe a strong diminution of propaganda distributed by tracts, unhappiness, anxiety, and irritation provoked by the inadequacies of supplies, terrorist attacks, and the police operations conducted by the authorities of the occupation have increased, because: at the onset of winter supplies have become scarcer; the terrorist attacks are more numerous, more audacious, and remain unpunished; the coercive measures taken by the German authorities have become harsher, often brutal. The disoriented, bitter, demoralized population, actively and skillfully worked by foreign or dissident radio propaganda, makes the government responsible for its sufferings. They reproach it with making itself the servile instrument of the occupier and more and more disrespect its authority. The great majority only expects salvation from the victory of the united Nations [the Allies] and each day they more and more turn toward the government in Algeria. Réfractaires and dissidents benefit from their sympathy, often finding aid and comfort among them. As for the terrorists, whose acts they do not always disapprove of and whose reprisals they fear, they assure them impunity with their complete mutism on everything concerning their actions and their hideouts. In a word, *the population, in its great majority, is no longer with the government. It is against the government and with the dissidents*. The calm that it continues to exhibit is only a prudent expectation, which could quickly turn if the occasion presented itself into a general agitation which would encompass not only the masses but also other classes, including those that formerly were the most fearful of the progress of Communism."[36]

The vocabulary used in the report speaks volumes: the popular Resistance offered its sympathy, aid, and comfort to resisters, assured their impunity by means of its absolute silence on everything concerning their actions and their safe havens. The commander of the gendarmerie even feared a general uprising (which in fact did not occur in the department[37]). The same report[38] mentions the "complicitous passivity of the population [who favor] the anti-National elements." The report of prefect Cousin,[39] January 3, 1944, specifies that "the populace distinguishes between réfractaires and terrorists, [it] is well-disposed toward the former but fears for the future because of the latter and it envisages the possibility of a civil war."[40]

Examples of the Workings and the Effectiveness of the Civilian Resistance of the Populace

From the end of 1942 the great majority of the population of the Drôme had turned away from the Vichy government, and a growing part of this population participated in the Resistance, bringing it aid, or their complicitous silence. They assured the logistics and supply services of the Resistance, whether military or political. They offered lodging and cover for clandestine resisters, for radio operators, for Jews, for those refusing to participate in the STO, for shotdown Allied aviators working their way to Spain, for the wounded of the undergrounds. They financed the Resistance. They rarely provided clothing, and never arms, which they nonetheless helped to hide.

In order to illustrate—and to confirm—the reports of the authorities, we will take two examples. One concerns geography, with the study of the Resistance in two communes in which "not much of importance happened"[41]: Mirmande and Saulce.[42] The other concerns a specific resistance activity: parachute drops.

Pierre de Saint-Prix, leader of the Drômian Resistance, originally hailed from Saulce-Mirmande. He writes[43]: "From 1942 an organization for concealing and hiding fighters sought by the police, as well as Jews, and later young people who wanted to escape the STO, functioned effectively. More than 1,500 réfractaires were transited at Mirmande, whether at the home of Louis Combe or the farm of Charles Caillet; what one had was a veritable 'dispatching' in which candidates were assigned to the farmers of the neighborhood. All of Mirmande resisted: Coste, the baker, Besson, the carpenter, Rouveyre, Bert, the café owner, Testu, Mr. and Mrs. Blanc, the secretary of the mayoralty and his wife, and so on. Marcelle Rivier sheltered Lövenstein, who, even while being of the Jewish faith, could live openly for a long time, and who was informed by the gendarmes of Loriol that Caillet had in his possession roundups ordered by Vichy." This idealized picture needs to be corrected. At the time, Mirmande contained 463 inhabitants.[44] There could not have been 1,500 réfractaires.

On her farm in Reys-de-Saulce, the mother of Mr. Dallard sheltered a cousin, a réfractaire from 1941 to 1943, who joined the underground, then another réfractaire from the end of 1943 to October 1944. The latter was also presented as a cousin to the soldiers of the German surveillance post of Logis-Neuf located 500 meters from the farm, kept by Germans and Poles, who often came to re-supply themselves there. Réfractaires were "placed" in Mirmande by Mr. Caillet, in Saulce by people and personalities of the municipality. It was necessary to convince people by showing that the réfractaire could work for the farmer, which wasn't always the case. Other witnesses indicate that there was only one réfractaire per farm, and that all the farms did not take in one. Mr. Bouyon, a former Saulceian resister, estimates the number of refugees or réfractaires in the farms of the two municipalities to be a hundred at most. To shelter someone required organization on the part of the family doing it. Their stays were therefore long, at least six months, always in the same place, because having the réfractaire move constituted a risk; and where would one send him? The Saulceian réfractaires who went to other municipalities to find refuge had the same problem.

Jewish refugees were disguised and hidden in the two communities. Pierre de Saint-Prix mentioned Mr. Lövenstein, whom Charles Caillet took to the abbey of Aiguebelle in February 1943, following a threat of arrest. Fred Samuel, "through the intermediary of Pastor Morin,[45] met Mrs. Courtin[46] who had the goodness to put at his disposal her house in Reys de Saulce. Other friends led him to the prefecture of Valence where new identity cards in the name of Soulas were produced…. Thus provided with false papers, the entire family rejoined him in the Reys de Saulce in March 1943…. Here, too, the population showed solidarity. The children were soon accepted. All the farmers helped as best they could. Sundays, they went to church. Once again, though, they had to watch their least action, in order not to arouse suspicion. They established contact with Mr. Caillet, mayor of Mirmande and head of the Resistance, whom they could not approach except with much caution. He was closely watched and no one could communicate with him except through the intermediary of women and children."[47] They could not raise any suspicion, because the inhabitants of Saulce didn't hide their anti-Semitism, but the latter "never did anything bad"[48] to them. A strong social pressure—at bottom, patriotic—exerted itself despite everything on those in the village where everyone knew everyone and where the partisans of the Resistance were in the majority. The structures of the Saulceian Resistance were served by the structures of solidarity, notably religious, which existed independently of the war (Catholic Help, Red Cross; Fred Samuel benefited from the network of Protestant assistance inspired by Pastor Morin). These structures served Jews, réfractaires from the STO, then members of the underground, as well as Alsacian or Toulonian refugees and needy families, especially those of prisoners of war.[49]

At the end of April the arrest of a Saulceian, a member of the Buckmaster-Roger network, by the Gestapo of Pont-Saint-Esprit, and the attempted arrest of Pierre de Saint-Prix by the Gestapo of Montélimar, led to the creation of a camp in the forest of Montélimar for five other Saulceians threatened with arrest; they were soon joined by other réfractaires. On June 6, 1944, some youth of the two communities joined the most determined of the réfractaires and fugitives and established an FFI company of the AS. "How, though, to feed everyone? Fruit, while abundant, wasn't adequate. It was necessary to seek a sheep, some chickens, at the farms. The signed slips of paper given in exchange didn't satisfy the farmers. Nonetheless, we

renewed the operation with tobacconists. How could we do anything differently? That lasted to the end of June. At that time the
success of the Allies encouraged the directors of supply depots to
pretty much supply us, from Montélimar."[50]

Parachute drops constitute our second example of the civilian
Resistance, that of the general populace, connected with the Resistance. A report of the gendarmerie is full of information concerning
the Allied parachute drops: "Multiple parachute drops of people, but
above all of material (posts of TSF, explosives, arms) were made by
British planes. Experience showed that drop zones of 250 meters
long and 150 meters wide were enough, if they were somewhat separate and isolated from the villages, pretty much [flat?], and without
enclosures or obstacles. The plane rarely landed (...picking up agents).
The materials, always dropped, included: cylinders filled with explosives, pistols, munitions, cigarettes, etc.... All the material, including containers, etc. was always immediately hidden on the spot, as
needed in a stream, and then gathered later. Sweeps of the area were
always done by police with powerful electric lights, led by accomplices or sympathizers of the locale. Parachute drops occurred just
about everywhere, especially in the free zone.... Everything occurred
during the new moon. That was the time when surveillance was the
greatest. Sometimes because of winds the landing on the ground of
the people or materials parachuted in occurred far enough from the
intended road or path. Current political circumstances allow one to
think that these parachute drops will multiply more and more. It is
necessary for us, therefore, to assure ourselves the help of trustworthy people living in the neighborhood of potentially serviceable terrain, in order to obtain information from them."[51] In April 1942 the
authorities of the Vichy government knew exactly what to take as
far as appropriate measures vis-à-vis well-established facts.

Now, in the Drôme no parachute drop-point was attacked during
the full-moon operations, neither by the French, nor the Germans
(nor the Italians). This was because it was not possible "to assure
themselves of the help of trustworthy people living in the neighborhood of potentially serviceable plots." Reports of the gendarmerie
speak of the seizure of containers, but always after the parachute drop.
If informers did exist beside the parachute drop-off points, the gendarmes often could not have the information followed through on.

The memoirs of Captain Alain (Pierre Raynaud) reveal that a parachute drop had many factors affecting its secrecy[52]: "Concerning

the organization of parachute drops: [P]ay attention to the quite frequent quarrels...the best agents often squabbled among themselves, there were problems of preeminence, of authority, of the distribution of parachutes, of shoes, of victuals, of cigarettes.... There were wives who didn't want to let their husbands go without an adequate explanation, who gossiped; in a word, there were all the problems posed by an immediate mobilization, for close to 24 hours, of at least twenty men, security, telephone lines to disconnect, commentaries to avoid—'What was the plane that passed overhead last night?'—'You will hear on the radio tonight that they will announce a bombardment of Italy.' [T]he botched rendezvous that didn't take place...finally waiting at the spot, ear to the ground to detect the oncoming...no, it's a truck, no, it's a motorbike, what can it be at this hour?... Then, it's him, a Halifax.... Say to the men: don't move when they are falling. Do not stop watching the plane in order to count the number of parachutes, and count them well; the plane will drop all the containers on the first pass, if none are caught in the bomb wells, then on the second the packets, then there will be a third pass if they have forgotten anything. Count them well, but pay attention that you don't catch one in the face (how did that almost never happen?).... It was very rare that all the parachutes were attached to their load. Roger [Francis Cammaerts] told me that it was Italian prisoners who 'fixed' our materials, and there was a very simple sabotage that consisted in not connecting the parachute to the container.

"We therefore received the two separately. It wasn't difficult folding the parachute, but on the other hand there were submachine guns to hide in the nooks and crannies.... [T]he plane, when it was British, left quietly on its last pass, after a little blinking of its lights. It was quickly done. If it was an American plane, it was a little different. No feints on the approach, no detours over a neighboring village in order to divert attention, no arrival at the site with the motors stilled and flying at low altitude in order to obtain a better grouping of the dropped items. No, as soon as the site was spotted, the plane went higher in order, one would say, to better survey the result: a dispersion area of four to five kilometers, because the release was made at high speed, with the necessary results.... Then when everything was spoiled, quite satisfied with himself the pilot descended at full speed...doubtlessly to prove to us that he saw us and that if he had launched everything far into nature, it wasn't his fault. When dawn arrived one was never sure to have found everything. One went back in order to have lunch...and then, without fail, with the sun already high, close to the house one would find, very high in the trees, two or three parachutes with striking colors. Then the reconstituted group would thrash about the entire country or mountain for kilometers around to find a few wanderers and to give to interlopers instructions to remain silent, reinforced by a Colt pistol or a Sten that had been parachuted in."

One should not consider the threat to interlopers mentioned above as adequate to dissuade anonymous denunciations, which would implicate so many people. The threat of repression by the Vichy authorities was very real, as a gendarmerie report shows, made after the first parachute drop of two Allied agents in Étoile: "A new fact in the area of antinational activity occurred in the department: On August 29, 1942, around one o'clock, two unidentified parachutists landed in the territory of the commune of Étoile on the Rhône. Two witnesses of this landing did not alert the gendarmerie until 7:30AM, when the two parachutists had long since disappeared. Despite searches immediately undertaken, they could not be found. The witnesses were arrested, in accordance with the Parquet, for having willingly failed to obstruct [the parachutists] and to indicate in a timely manner an antinational activity (Law of 29.7.1881, art. 33)."[53]

In conclusion: [this was] a clandestine activity that was barely hid and was known to many. The examples nicely reveal the support, the complicity, of the population with the Resistance.

These two examples confirm the terms used by the commander of the gendarmerie of the Drôme in his report of December 1943. The structures and the activities of the Resistance, whether they concerned Saulece-Mirmande or the parachute drops, were squarely based on those—structures and activities—of the society.

The same thing is observed in a certain number of other communes: at Nyons, around the team of Dr. Bourdongle, at Dieulefit around Marguerite Soubeyran's, at Crest with Hérold's, at Saint-Donat and the team of the pharmacist Chancel and his father-in-law, Dr. Lémonon, and at Grant-Serre with Alfred Lesage.[54] All of them asked their circle of relatives and relations to participate in some manner in the Resistance. In this circle the first to be solicited were the family members, notably the wives. We have already mentioned the Lémonons-Chancels. At Romans, André Vincent-Beaume conducted his Resistance activities with the total support of his wife and sons. At Portes-lès-Valence, the parents of René Ladet informed him, fed

him, and hid him; he escaped from German-occupied Die at the end
of July 1944 with his sister and his fiancée. At Montélimar it was the
entire Grouiller family that published *Liberation*, and all were arrested by the Gestapo in December 1943. Mrs. Grouiller did not
return from deportation. We mentioned the mother of René Courtin
at Saulce; at Die, his wife "made his estate a sort of Thébaïde where
unfortunate Jewish children were sheltered and hidden, in particular
the orphans of the Hamff and Bloch families, and where numerous
resisters could find comfort and information."[55] It was especially in
the "familial" mode that the Resistance of women occurred. They
occupy a fundamental place in the "unrecognized resistance."

Reality of the Engagement of the Civilian Resistance
of the Population

For the general population life continued during the war.
Resistance's "availability," the risks and sacrifices, the activities for
which it was ready-and-willing, were a function of that fact as much
as of factors tied to the personality of each individual, as well as
those found in his familial and social environment.

The majority of the population, unlike the underground, couldn't
hide and couldn't emigrate. Nonetheless, its assistance to the Resistance was often quite prompt, whether it concerned something on-
going or a specific action. As we already have said, this participation in the Resistance was not without its risks.

The repression exercised by the Vichy government[56] or by the
Italians[57] was often measured. Not so with the Germans. From the
time of their installation in the Drôme, the Germans intervened in
Romans in reprisal for the strike of September 20, 1943: "54 people
in all were arrested, 26 still retained on November 3,"[58] who will be
deported; only ten of them will return.

After the theft of telephone wire by the Geyer-Thivollet underground at Grand-Serre in September, on October 9, "at daybreak,
the Germans encircled the village of Grand-Serre, and proceeded to
arrest mayor Alfred Lesage and his family, as well as the senior war-
rant officer of the gendarmerie who protected the Geyer underground,
two members of the Geyer underground who were returning from a
mission to Lyon, and several other people. Several were deported or
jailed at Lyon."[59] On December 27, 1943, in the villages of Vercheny,
Pontaix, Barsac, and Sainte-Croix, eighty men were arrested, fifty-

six deported, in reprisal for an attack against a train of German soldiers on leave December 22 at Vercheny. One of the authors of the
assault was among the prisoners, but he was not betrayed by the
others. Arrests effected after police inquiry (often because of betrayals) were better "targeted," for example at Saoû, when on May 20,
1944 the Germans took "René and Yvonne Mure (baker), Gabriel
Gontard (mayor), Plumel (field hand), Henri François (postmaster),
Justin Bayle, René Cavagne, Antonin Desseigne, Reine Eymery,
Fragnol, Magnet, Flavien Vigne, and André Viret. After these arrests, '[the people] finally saw the light [regarding the Germans]' in
Saoû."[60] This isn't totally correct: "[A]t the moment when the prisoners taken by the Germans were being loaded, René Mure heard
someone, a Pétainist of the village, say in a loud voice, 'I know very
well that they [the Germans] won't do anything to us, because we
others haven't done anything.'"[61]

It was above all after June 6, 1944 that the repression became
savage: in addition to executions, there were a hundred rapes at Saint-
Donat on June 15, and twice as many at Crest on July 20, two towns
that had done much for the Resistance.

The German reprisals, as we just saw, not only affected those who
participated in the Resistance. A part of the populace felt—at the
least—a certain bitterness at being thus caught in a conflict whose
negative consequences they wanted to avoid. Those who continued
to take the risk of aiding the Resistance during the battles of June,
July, and August 1944 have that much more merit. When Captain
Planas had to re-supply his underground after the "cleansing" of
Vercors in July, farmers (one of whom was a former hunting buddy[62])
gave him food for his hundred men. Others partially assumed this
risk. When the Germans attacked Combovin June 22, 1944, one of
the farmers who sheltered the underground "covered his ass" by
writing on the walls of his house that the underground had taken it
over by force. Some did not assume any risks at all and sometimes it
was the weapons of the underground that convinced them to do so.

However, the effect of these forces in general led the population, as
we have seen, to be largely favorable to the Allies and the Resistance.
The Germans may have had a veritable fear of this populace: several
witnesses recount that the Germans, during their retreat at the end of
August 1944, made *them* eat the food prepared for the Germans.[63]

This distrust of the enemy is a testimony to the civilian Resistance
of the populace, who were recognized and thanked by all the politi-

cal and military leaders of the Resistance in the Drôme. All the latter's
works or testimonials underscore it. For example, Alexis Santini, an
officer in the Air Force, was posted to Crupies in February 1943.
There he formed an underground in 1944. He speaks of "these working peasants, courageous and patriotic, who in every circumstance
showed [him] their entire solidarity."[64] When he arrived at Valence
in February 1944, General de Lassus lodged with Mr. and Mrs.
Gachon, who doubted that "he was employed by the Rivers and
Forests department as he told them. They knew therefore the risks
they were running, but they were admirable patriots."[65]

On the administrative plane this Resistance was less well recognized. Of the 2,300 CVR cards issued in the Drône, very few men
and women obtained them because of an "interior Resistance" (undertaken outside of a Resistance organization) or an "isolated Resistance." After a scrutiny of a sample of 900 CVRs, we were able to
find only four men and one woman in these categories. People from
Mirmand and Saulce referred to by Pierre de Saint-Prix in his book
saw their request denied. Perhaps the category of "combatant" cannot be attributed to those who practiced this form of resistance.

A Very Real Nebula

As the sum of uncoordinated, small individual actions, to which
were added or progressively substituted participation in the organized structures of the Resistance supported by the majority of the
population, the Resistance doesn't have exact geographic, political,
or religious contours. But geography, politics, and religion shape its
contours in accordance with the times and events. Thus this system
that was the Resistance was formed and evolved. In a nebula the
stars are not everywhere. But everywhere there are stars. In the
Drôme, as in the rest of France, the Resistance wasn't everywhere,
but everywhere saw the Resistance. The example of this district,
which saw all the forms of resistance, illustrates very well the "unrecognized resistance" about which Jacques Debû-Bridel spoke.

Notes

1.   The Drôme administrative district is found in the southeast of France.
2.   Daughter of Dr. Lémonon, the wife of the pharmacist of Saint-Donat; the two will
be the heads of the Resistance of the commune and will take part in the hiding of
Jews andréfractaires, in a network of escape and evasion for Allied pilots, in the
OSS Azur network for which they organized parachute drops. Her brother, Michel

Lémonon, a Catholic priest, will give a speech against Nazism on April 9, 1942 in the town.

3. Testimony of Mady Chancel in Matthäus Schindele, *Saint-Donat—Ein Zentrum des Widerstandes 1940-1944* (self-published, 1996), pp. 7-9; and Fr. Michael Lémonon, *Laurent ou l'itinéraire d'un prêtre ouvrier*, p. 89.

4. Sandrine Suchon, *Résistance et liberté, Dieulefit 1940-1944* (éditions à Die, 1994), p. 41. F-G Dreyfus adds concerning Pastor Boegner, that he was "a great Protestant, who also was a great Frenchman, who undeniably had more than sympathy for the national Revolution and Marshal Pétain, even if he clearly condemned the policy of Vichy." See his *Histoire de la Résistance* (de Fallois, 1996), p. 328.

5. Socialist and Freemason, shot by the Germans at the end of July 1944, after having been made a prisoner at the evacuation of Vercors.

6. *Drôme Nord, terre d'asile et de révolte* (Peuple Libre, 1993), p. 121.

7. Historical service of the national gendarmerie, Report Cie Drôme R4, n. 32/4 of September 28, 1940.

8. Drôme PCF Archives, tract of October 16, 1991. We know that "the appeal of July 10" was after that date.

9. SHGN, report Cie Drôme R4, n. 51/4 of October 28, 1940. Anti-national propaganda.

10. Grouped around the young Socialist Roger Coursange, who conducted in the Drôme and Ardèche all forms of Resistance until August 1944, when he was grievously wounded in an engagement with the Germans. At the end of June 1941, four member of a "group of hoodlums," including Coursange, were arrested.

11. AN side F/1CIII/1152, prefect report of November 11, 1940, pp. 21-22.

12. *Drôme Nord, terre d'asile et de révolte*, op. cit., p. 28.

13. Report of the prefect of the Drôme, December 12, 1940, AN F/1cIII/1152, pp. 17, 20-23.

14. As the prefect shows in his report of December 19, 1940; he indicates that after the arrival of the Lorrainian refugees, "Gauleiter Burckel's proclamation, despite its rather eloquent style, gave everyone the opportunity of concluding 'that they still were the same.' It will be very difficult to change the impression made by this proclamation." Several later reports move in the same direction. German propaganda will provoke great hostility in the Drôme against the Germans after the first repressions in 1943.

15. Testimony in the periodical *Dauphiné libéré*, August 18, 1998 and August 24, 1998.

16. Notably in the region of Beaurepaire. It was written on these tracts: "Courage, Belgian friends, England fights to deliver you, and it will win" (in Suzanne Sylvestre, *Revue d'histoire de la 2eme Guerre mondiale*, n. 127, p. 57, citing AD Isère 4Z44).

17. Henri Amouroux, *Le people réveillé* (Robert Laffont, 1979), p. 260.

18. SHGN, report R4 Cie Drôme n. 86/4 of June 19, 1941. A document concerning Gaullist propaganda.

19. SHGN, report R4 Cie Drôme n. 103-4 of July 18, 1941. Information concerning Gaullist activity. The two towns are found in central Drôme: Saillans is to the east of Crest and Bourdeaux close to Dieulefit.

20. SHGN, report R2 Section Die n. 66/2 of March 4, 1941.

21. In February the prefect demanded his transfer.

22. SHGN, report R4 Section Crest n. 103/4 of October 23, 1941.

23. Paul Pons, *De la Résistance à la Libération* (self-published, 1962), p. 15, confirmed by SHGN, report R4 Section Crest n. 115/4 of December 15, 1941.

24. For military resistance, such as that connected to the CDM, clandestinity went without saying from June 25, 1940.

25.   ADD 248W5, sub-prefect of Nyons, report of December 20, 1941, p. 2.

26.   The government, but not Marshal Pétain, whose standing remained high in public opinion. As Paxton wrote in *La France de Vichy* (Seuil, 1997), p. 25: "public opinion constantly distinguished between Pétain and his government" and all authors agree concerning the popularity of the Marshal; even in May 1943 the commander of the gendarmerie of the Drôme wrote that "he is still uniformly respected, but his prestige and his authority seem to lessen a good deal, most people currently say that he no longer has any real power" (report R4 n. 37/4 of May 24, 1943). See also Pierre Laborie, *L'opinion française sous Vichy* (Seuil, 1990).

27.   SHGN, report R4 Section Die n. 39/4 of August 1, 1942, then n. 45/4 of August 19, 1942.

28.   Legislation of the Occupation, v. X, Oct-December 1942, Press of the Palace, Paris, p. 160.

29.   Others will do both, and the rifle will be the cause of their death. On March 9, 1944, at Sainte-Euphémie, the Germans did not find any members of the underground but they found hunting rifles belonging to the Jarjaye family who supported the underground. The father and three sons were shot.

30.   Then the STO (obligatory work service in Germany) in January 1943.

31.   Romans is a town where the Resistance was very active throughout the war; strikes and demonstrations took place there against the STO in March and September 1943. The March demonstration was organized by the Christian Working Youth and the Communist Youth. That of September is the work of the United Movements of the Resistance (MUR).

32.   Lémonon, *Jean Perriolat, témoin du Christ en STO* (Deval, 1989), p. 23.

33.   Sandrine Suchon, op. cit., p. 81.

34.   Cf. *Le Monde*, January 21, 2000, p. 14, article by Philipp Broussard on "El Chico" Klein: "When Georges Klein's parents settled in the Drôme in 1938, it was to flee the Nazis who just invaded their country, Austria. This Jewish family first fled to Paris, then to Romans, where it had the luck of escaping the roundups. Rodolphe, the father, took so little care to hide himself that he opened a leather-goods store. 'They never had the least problem' assures his brother-in-law.'"

35.   AN side F/1CIII/1152, report of the prefect of January 1, 1943.

36.   SHGN, report Cie Drome R4, n. 113/4 of December 27, 1943, a view of the whole. The italicized passages are ours.

37.   Nor were there insurrections.

38.   In the chapter "Anti-national Propaganda."

39.   Very favorable to the Resistance, who will accomplish several acts of resistance on his own initiative and in the context of his position. Very connected with the members of the NAP, he will be arrested and deported in May 1944.

40.   AN side F/1CIII/1152, prefect report of January 3, 1944, public opinion.

41.   This characterization is repeated by several witnesses.

42.   Communes that were one until 1860. They are found fifteen kilometers north of Montélimar, on national Route 7, along the Rhône.

43.   In *Combats pour le Vercors et pour la Liberté* (Peuple Libre, 1984), pp. 168ff.

44.   Children included; the number of prisoners of war is unknown. Saulce contained nineteen. This commune, which Pierre de Saint-Prix forgets, then only had 1,053 inhabitants.

45.   Pastor Morin lived in Cliousclat, a neighboring town.

46.   Mother of René Courtin, one of the leaders of the Combat movement.

47.   Fred, *Mémoires d'un joaillieer* (Le Rocher, 1992), pp. 106-108.

48.   Testimony of Mr. Briançon, head of the local Committee for the Liberation of Saulce, collected in March 1996.

49. See our dissertation for the DEA, *La Résistance dans le departement de la Drôme 1940-1944* (Université Paris IV-Sorbonne, May 1997), pp. 107-140.

50. Fred, *Mémoires d'un joaillier*, pp. 111-112. Fred Samuel, former legionnaire, was then head-sergeant of this company.

51. SHGN, report Cie Drome R4, n. 29-4 of April 21, 1942.

52. ADD, FFI files 97J27, pp. 299-305.

53. SHGN, report Cie Drome R4, n. 137/4 of September 24, 1942.

54. Their points in common were patriotism, humanism, and attachment to the Republic. From philosophic or religious points of view, they could be secular, Catholic, Protestant, Freemasons; politically one finds men of the "left" and the "right."

55. Jean Veyer, *Souvenirs de la Résistance dioise* (self-published, 1986), p. 30.

56. An exception: the executions and arrests done by the militia, especially during its operations against Vercors in April 1944.

57. The Italian repression in the Drôme lacks a common measure with the German or militia repressions. Italian authorities even intervened with the prefect, to release the Jews he had arrested at the beginning of 1943.

58. AN side F/1CIII/1152, prefect's report of November 3, 1943, who adds that "these facts have caused a very strong emotion."

59. *Pour l'amour de la France* (Peuple Libre), p. 165. Twelve people were arrested. In August the Vichy authorities had tried to neutralize the Geyer underground. Without success…. The report destined for the prefect underlines that the "group of one hundred men is supplied by the people of the country [and it benefits] from the most complete complicity on the part of the population." AN F/1a/3901 and 3AG2/478-171Mi189.

60. Henri Fuoc, *Histoire de Saoû* (manuscript, 1998), p. 2.

61. The weekly, *Le Crestois*, July 15, 1994, testimony of René Mure. The persons who were arrested were helping the underground concealed in the woods of the commune.

62. Captain Planas was a Catholic, his friend a Protestant.

63. As far as we know, no German soldier died of poisoned food in the Drôme.

64. Testimony published in the review *Icare* 1994/1, p. 49.

65. General de Lassus-Saint-Geniès, *Combats pour le Vercors et pour la liberté* (Peuple libre, 1984), p. 39.

Testimonies and Testimonials

Remarks of Ambassador Vernon Walters

It is a great honor to have been invited to speak to those who never lost their faith. Their faith in the role of France as a great power, a role it has played for a thousand years.

My first contact with France occurred when I arrived here in 1923, at the age of six. I still remember that after only two or three days my mother said, "We are going to send you to school here." I said, "But mom, I do not speak French." She smiled and said, "You will learn to speak French very quickly and very well because you will be pressured by the French children. Ridicule is more important to children than to adults when they have to learn a foreign language." Since then I have spent a total of twenty-nine years of my life in France, ten as a child and nineteen as an adult, in various posts.

I went to war and arrived in North Africa on November 8 [no year provided]. We were helped a great deal by the French Resistance. For example, one of my duties was "to kidnap" the operators of the Safi harbor. I already had their addresses and their hotel room numbers. I went to nab them. They all came voluntarily. None ever complained. They asked, "Is it a commando?" I said, "No, it is not a commando." There were hundreds of thousands of soldiers who came to help us.

I will speak, if I may, on two different subjects. The first is the relationship between General de Gaulle and General Eisenhower, in which I was very closely involved. In the United States I remember having heard "the appeal" of General de Gaulle. The sentence that impressed me the most was: "France has lost a battle, but not the war."

I enrolled in the army before our entry into the war because I saw the war coming. We were too important a country to escape history. It was clear that we would have to participate in this war. In fact Mr. Roosevelt soon understood that it was impossible to let the Nazis win the war. This very great man, like all great men, had a weakness: he had the impression that General de Gaulle was like a Latin American general who would come to power with the Allied forces, set himself up, and stay there forever.

It was a complete misunderstanding not shared by the people. If you strolled down Fifth Avenue during the war you would have seen in the shops a portrait of General de Gaulle. To Mr. Roosevelt the general seemed a very rigid man, but he had to be rigid, otherwise France would not have kept her role as a great power—a role that France occupied until the time that de Gaulle left the government. Wherever the French forces were you would hear, "What is de Gaulle going to say? How is he going to receive it? What is he going to do?"

Generals de Gaulle and Eisenhower met when Eisenhower went to London from North Africa. Eisenhower knew perfectly well that the immense majority of the French favored de Gaulle and the French Resistance.

When I returned to the United States for a debriefing at the Pentagon someone asked me, "What's going on over there? What is the public opinion?" I said, "It is that France will reenter the war and the French see de Gaulle as the head of the Resistance. They see only him." They said, "But there is General Giraud." So I answered, "Everybody admires General Giraud and his escape from Germany at his age, but he is not seen as the incarnation of a reborn France." I was a second lieutenant at that time and was told, "Be prudent, do not say this too loud." But I said it very loudly. It was a blind spot with Roosevelt, one that I never understood. I don't know who gave him these ideas. However, there it was.

Such was definitely not the case with General Eisenhower. I met him while leaving North Africa; I went to England in order to return to the United States. He received me and said, "You have lived there and you speak French well." He asked about public opinion. I answered, "The opinion is *gaulliste*. It is General de Gaulle who will be the head of the French government after the liberation of France." He then said to me, "According to all the indications of our information services you are correct."

Information, as you know, was of extreme importance to the Resistance. We knew—we, the Allies—we knew what was happening in France practically as well as anyone who lived in France or the Germans themselves.

I saw General de Gaulle for the first time in London because I brought him a letter from General Béthouart. General Béthouart had tried to help our landing at Casablanca but was arrested by Admiral Fénard. I went to Algeria with General Béthouart and I brought his letter to de Gaulle in London. He asked me where I had learned French. I explained to him and when I told him that I was going back to the United States he said, "That's too bad, we could have used you here."

I left, but upon arriving in the United States I realized that what I wanted most at that time, promotions and decorations, could not happen on this side of the Atlantic, and it was necessary that I return to the war. So, I arranged to return to the war. It was evident to me from the few contacts I had in London that there was already practically a government organized. Speaking with the Americans and the British it was clear that they had all sorts of contacts in France and knew perfectly what was happening in the entirety of the country and that they were not worried about the attitude of the French people.

The French army in Italy had reestablished the confidence of the Anglo-Americans in the fighting power of the French soldiers. These soldiers, who had fought in Tunisia and Italy, reestablished in the minds of the Americans and the British the fact that the French were still fine soldiers and were only asking to prove it. And they proved it.

We knew that there was another French army that was fighting, with Eisenhower and de Gaulle and with de Gaulle and the Americans. General de Gaulle came after the campaign of Italy to discuss the landing of Provence. He was received by General Clark, whose aide-de-camp I was at the time.

In London I was told that General de Gaulle did not speak English. I was still young and innocent and I believed what I read in the newspapers: General de Gaulle does not speak English. Therefore during the conversation that unfolded General Clark several times answered, "No." De Gaulle asked me, "What did he say?" I explained to him, "He said, 'non' Mon Général." Convinced that he did not understand one word of English, I added things here and there, such as "General de Gaulle said 'yes,' but I do not think that he wants to do it." Or "I think that General de Gaulle said, 'no,' but if you insist a little, he will say yes."

Then, at a certain moment when they were discussing the landing of Provence, General Clark insisted that I be included. At that point,

General de Gaulle looked at General Clark and said, "Isn't it a bit strange that you, an American general, tell me who must command the French army that will land in France? I also have General de Tassigny who has been fighting inside France and I will use him." And when we were leaving he said to me in English, "Walters, it is all right, but don't do that too often." I never did it again the rest of my life.

After, there was a long interval. General Eisenhower returned to Europe as Commander of NATO. It was hard to see General de Gaulle, who at that point was the chief opponent of the French government which was lodging Eisenhower at a beautiful villa at Marnes-la-Coquete. Finally, their encounter took place at the Hôtel de l'Ordre de la Libération in Paris, on rue François 1.

After lunch we went into the garden. There were three chairs: one for de Gaulle, one for Eisenhower, and one for me (it was 1952). General de Gaulle said to Eisenhower, "Both of us, we will be called to run our countries, you before me. When I come back, I will have to do certain things that will be disagreeable to you. I have to give back to the French people the feeling of the grandeur of their country, and of the fact that they cannot count on others to safeguard them. They must do it themselves and organize it themselves. By means of words, I will use the crop on them. When you hear these words, know why I do it." General Eisenhower said to me, "He is a strange man, an extraordinary man." He had profound admiration for de Gaulle and it was reciprocal. (Although he was an American subordinate receiving Roosevelt's orders which enormously displeased him, he executed them the least he could.) Later on de Gaulle was the first head of state to say that he would attend Eisenhower's funeral, which obliged all the others to come.

Up to the end there was a close relationship between them. I remember one of Eisenhower's visits. He disembarked from his plane. I was behind him in case there was need of an interpreter. General de Gaulle always had an interpreter, but didn't need one. I learned this in Italy, when he said in English, "Don't do that too often" (one of the few times I heard him speak in English). Eisenhower got down from his plane and de Gaulle looked at him and said, "You are welcome, for whatsoever happens you will always be for us the commander-in-chief of the years of liberation." I saw tears in Eisenhower's eyes. He said to me, "He is a true friend."

The second proof happened during the U-2 meeting, when an American plane was brought down over Russia [1960]. General de Gaulle presided in his role as host. Khrushchev asked to speak and de Gaulle said to him, "The only head of State beside myself is General Eisenhower," to which Khrushchev replied, "I asked first." He then got up and read a letter that said if the Americans didn't apologize he would leave and not come back. He then left.

There was a kind of general panic. Nobody knew what to say. Then de Gaulle took both Eisenhower and me by the elbow into a corner. He said, "I don't know what he is going to do, I don't know what will happen, but whatever happens we will be with you till the end."

Right there I had the confirmation of a fact that I had often observed (please excuse my language): "The French and the Americans fight all the time when nothing very serious is at stake, but for two hundred and fifty years every time serious matters occur we are always on the same side of the ramparts."

This relationship has been very important in maintaining France's role as a great power. There evidently was a giant that directed France's destiny, and there was also the Resistance.

Perhaps the Resistance did not win the war but it decided [the issue of] the honor of France. It proved that inside a defeated France there were always some forces wanting to resist, forces that wanted to change what had happened. These maintained the honor of this great country. All the Americans, British, and members of the OSS, all knew that the immense majority of the French people, even if they didn't take to the street to demonstrate, were against the Occupation, against the defeat, and wanted to change things. We were deeply aware of this resistance.

When I was ambassador to Germany I often asked the Germans if they were aware of the attitude of the French. They replied, "Yes, when we entered a restaurant, a cold atmosphere enveloped us. Nobody would give us change. Nobody knew where the Arc de Triomphe or Notre Dame was. We could profoundly feel, if not the hostility, the coldness of the people."

This resistance was repressed in an extraordinarily savage way. And probably by doing this they nourished the Resistance, to the point of provoking this song, composed in part by my friend Maurice Druon. We were always struck by the "bloody" quality of "The Marseillaise." First of all by the extraordinary music, but also the bloody words. The "Chant des Partisans" is even bloodier: *Friends, do you hear over our planes, the dark flight of the crows? Tonight the enemy will know the price of blood and of tears.*

I know that this also lives in your heart and it expressed this immense country's extraordinary resistance, because you are the largest country in Europe after Russia. It was this resistance that nourished all that we did before the landing, afterwards, and during all of the advance across France.

I hope that now that some time has passed histories of the Resistance such as Professor Dreyfus has written will be published in the United States. Perhaps abridged, perhaps less detailed, but it is necessary for people to understand: All those who were saved by the Resistance, all the pilots who were led to Spain, or those who were hidden, all these people will never forget.

As for myself, who loves France, I believe that this Resistance had a direct, immediate, and lasting effect on the fact that France is still a great power after a thousand years. France survived the defeat of 1940, and today is still a great power. Thank you.

The Medal of the Resistance

Jean-Jacques de Bresson

Ladies and Gentlemen, I have to say that the expositions that I heard this morning gave me a good deal of pleasure, especially that of Alain Griotteray who opened the colloquium. I believe that one should retain one main thing from it: that the French people did not fall prostrate before the German occupation. It is true that today— and it really isn't only recently—certain people portray the morale of the French as at its lowest in 1939. And from that one naturally draws the conclusion that France in 1940 accepted willingly the presence of the enemy. For this reason it is good to recall certain facts and that was done this morning. But I wish to emphasize several.

During the military campaign of 1939-1940 French soldiers proved themselves during the cruel period that unfolded from May 10 to the Armistice. During that period the French army fought hard. For proof one has the figure of 100,000 dead. I believe that there were more deaths during this campaign than during the battle of the Marne in 1914. And on another hand, it should not be forgotten that regarding our aviation, which is so often denigrated, our planes and pilots shot down between eight and nine hundred German planes which the Luftwaffe sorely missed during the battle of Britain. I believe that these are things that need to be remembered.

From them I draw the conclusion that the French people weren't totally beaten down in 1940 and, after a period of stupefaction that obviously followed the quick collapse of our forces, the French people were receptive enough to hear the historical "appeal" of General de Gaulle. Of course, to claim that all the French resisted except for those that General de Gaulle called "a handful of miserable human beings" would be to say too much. But I very sincerely believe,

---

Jean-Jacques de Bresson is president of the National Association of the Holders of the Medal of the French Resistance.

and I believe it from personal experience, that the Resistance, embryonic in 1940 of course, was able to develop because the French people took to it like a fish to water, according to a famous formulation we heard this morning.

I believe that all of that is very important to retain. I believe that what must be transmitted to the younger generations is that with respect to the older generation of the war they need never have either sorrow or pity. The latter words were used deliberately, apropos to a film, *The Sorrow and the Pity*, that people tried at the time I was general director of the ORTF to have me show on television. I formally refused. Many criticized me for refusing. I believe that I was right to think that this film did not present an accurate view of what France was during the war. That is the first thing.

The second thing I would like to say, even though I don't want to monopolize the time, is that we all knew that the French Resistance was something involving the French populations of almost all the regions of the country. I am the national president of the Holders of the Medal of the French Resistance and I would say that in this capacity I have a fairly exact view of the way in which the French conducted themselves during the war. And what is striking to see is that the Resistance, if it didn't have the same intensity in every region, was found everywhere.

As proof I cite the fact that in addition to particular individuals, for whom it is more difficult to identify the exact locale where they performed their acts of resistance, the medal of the Resistance was awarded to seventeen territorial collectivities. We have in France seventeen territorial collectivities and more than a dozen moral "persons" who have received the medal of the Resistance. And we have an overseas territory, New Caledonia, which rallied very quickly to the Free French. I further should say that when one looks at the map of those communities that received the medal of the Resistance one sees two things. First, they go from great cities such as Lyon or Brest to the smallest municipalities, such as Ile de Sein, and even further to the small villages that distinguished themselves during the war.

According to what criteria was the medal awarded? It is at this point that we reconnect with our purpose here today. They were awarded to the communities that particularly suffered because of their populations' affirmative attitude toward the Resistance. Of the various populations that provided supplies to the undergrounds I will only speak about Lyon. Lyon was the city that as everyone knows harbored the great movements of the Resistance—as some have said, Lyon was the capital of the Resistance. But I think also of the small communities that were sprinkled over the country from Travaux in Aisne to Terrou in Lot or Plougasnou in North Finistère. And in fact these communities all suffered cruelly during the war. Their populations, because they aided the Resistance, drew upon themselves terrible reprisals on the part of the Germans.

I think of the village of Marsoulas found in the confines of Ariège and of Haute Garonne where almost the entire population was shot and even infants in the crib were massacred. When we speak of the nebulous mist that surrounded the Resistance, the "unrecognized resistance," those populations are a perfect illustration. It was not great leaders who fell but populaces who believed it was their duty to aid the Resistance.

I am not going to say more at this point, but I simply would like to confirm in my capacity as president of the Holders of the Medal of the French Resistance the views expressed and laid out earlier this morning. I thank you.

Testimonial of Ralph Patton

First, I would like to thank the members of the bureau and all the members of the Club Témoin for the invitation to speak at this colloquium.

The forgotten men and women of the French Resistance have been very dear to my heart since January 5, 1944, when my B-17 was shot down by German FW 190s a few kilometers from Lorient. The raison d'être of the Air Forces Escape and Evasion Society, founded in 1964, is to commemorate the men and women who risked their lives in order to save ours.

The 8th Air Force started operations in June 1942. Between that time and the end of the war in May 1945, over 60,000 of its airmen were downed over western Europe, 2,600 were killed, and 30,000 were taken prisoner. Thanks to the Resistance over 4,000 members of the 8th Air Force were able to evade capture and return to Allied territory.

Even though we never wanted to acknowledge it, crews of the 8th Air Force knew that they had a huge chance of being shot down. We also knew that most French people were sympathetic to the Allies and that they would willingly help downed airmen, but no one told us that organized escape networks actually existed. The return of an airman who had been shot down had an electrifying effect on the morale of the crews still flying combat.

At noon on January 5, 1944 seven of our crew parachuted from our crippled B-17G. Unfortunately, three of ours had been killed. We were returning to England after having bombed the German airfield at Mérignac, near Bordeaux.

Ralph Patton is chairman of the Air Forces Escape and Evasion Society, which he co-founded with Leslie Atkinson of Paris in 1964. The purpose of the Society is to encourage U.S. evaders to renew and retain relationships with the men and women of the Resistance. Patton was the copilot of a B-17 shot down over western France on January 5, 1944. He was hidden by his French helpers for sixty-two days and then evacuated to England via British MGB 502 on March 18, 1944.

I opened my parachute at 8,000 feet and landed safe and sound in front of a farmhouse where a farmer and his wife had seen the FW 190s attack our airplane. Unable to speak or understand a word of French, I could not communicate with the farmer or his wife, so I ran to hide myself in a nearby forest. I later learned that the farmer picked up my parachute and hid it and then told the Germans that he had not seen any airmen. I believe that that is the first, and least recognized, manifestation of the French Resistance. Thousands of French knew where the pilots were but they said nothing to the hated Gestapo.

Within minutes of landing I had the good fortune to meet up with our first pilot, Glenn Johnson, and Jack McGough, our bombardier. The three of us walked in an easterly direction until about 4:30 in the afternoon. When it began to get cold and dark we decided that we had to approach someone for help. After watching an isolated farmhouse for fifteen minutes we decided to try our luck. Désiré Gerone answered our vigorous knocking on his door with a puzzled expression on his face and a hesitant invitation for us to come in and sit by the open fire.

By sign language we were able to make Désiré, his mother, and brother understand that we were American airmen from the plane that had been shot down that afternoon. His mother prepared a large tureen of hot soup while Désiré opened a bottle of his best wine.

A little after we finished eating the brother prepared to go out and made us understand that he would soon return. We had no idea why he was leaving, but the warmth of their welcome took away all fear that he was going to hand us over to the Gestapo.

We were quite comfortable sitting beside a warm fire, having had a bowl of soup and several glasses of wine. When the brother returned he motioned to us that we should follow him outside. Fifteen minutes of walking brought us to a large two-story house where we were greeted by Lucien Denmat and his wife. After an hour of strained sign language conversation we were served coffee and cookies and then led up to the second floor where each of us was directed to his own bedroom. On our first night in France we were privileged to sleep in down-filled comforters on a full stomach, our minds put at ease by several glasses of wine.

After a good night's sleep and a hearty breakfast, Mr. Denmat pointed us in an easterly direction and wished us "Bonne chance." Unfortunately, Mr. Denmat had no connection with any group of the organized resistance; in fact he didn't know any. I believe that he and his wife constitute a second level of the French Resistance: ready to help, but without any ties to the active Resistance.

On our second night in France we tried to sleep in a field under the open sky but it was too cold so we walked most of the night. It was easier walking at night; one could safely walk on the roads, and the only hazard was barking dogs.

Shortly after noon on our second day we were stopped by a teacher who motioned for us to follow him. While standing in the middle of the road trying to communicate with the teacher we spotted a gendarme on a bicycle about 100 meters from us, headed in our direction.

It was obvious that the gendarme had seen us, so all we could do was await his arrival. The gendarme and the teacher had an animated conversation for a few minutes and then the gendarme shook his head, seemingly in disbelief, mounted his bicycle and headed up the road.

By sign language the teacher told us that he did not think the gendarme would report us to the Germans, but he was not certain, so we had better stay off the road and walk through the fields. He led us to a hiding place on a height near the Nantes-to-Brest canal, where he told us to remain until his return. We were warned not to move around much as there was a German observation tower on the hill across the canal.

Shortly after dark the teacher returned with his wife, who brought a large tureen of hot soup. After we had eaten what we considered to be gourmet soup, the teacher led us to the edge of the borough of Plelauff, where there was a haystack about twenty meters from a farmhouse. He pushed aside the front of the haystack to reveal a large opening within. After he saw the three of us comfortably installed in the center of the haystack, he indicated that he would return in the morning.

Just as we were about asleep we were aroused by the barking of a very excited dog. After about ten minutes of continuous barking the farmer came to find out why his dog was so excited. The farmer parted the hay and shined his lantern directly onto our sleepy faces. In unison we shouted "Americans, Americans." With a comprehending look on his face the farmer covered up the opening in the hay, took his dog by the collar, and led him back to the farm. Ten minutes later the farmer was back with a bottle of Calvados and a loaf of bread.

Before dawn the next morning the teacher arrived with bread and hardboiled eggs for our breakfast and then led us through the borough of Plelauff. The schoolteacher apparently was still apprehensive because of our chance meeting with the gendarme of the day before and decided that it was too dangerous for him to continue to occupy himself with us. As we parted company he gave us a map and suggested that perhaps the brothers of the Abbey de Langonnet, about twenty kilometers from there, would help us. I never did learn the name of the teacher from Plelauff. Apparently the gendarme did not report his encounter with the Americans.

Before the teacher left us we had met two more American airmen alongside the road. Despite the darkness I was able to recognize Isadore Viola, our gunner. The other man was Lt. Norman King, navigator from another B-17 that had been shot down at almost the same time as ours. We were now five American airmen wandering around in the center of Brittany with a price of 10,000 francs on each of our heads.

Shortly after noon on the third day we arrived near the town of Plouay, population 2,000. We knew that we couldn't walk through the center of town in broad daylight, so we circled the town on the west side by walking through farms. We climbed over many hedgerows and crossed many streams before we reached the main road south out of Plouray, en route to the Abbey de Langonnet.

Lucien Quillot, an eleven-year-old boy, spotted the five of us as we came back on the road. When he was late in returning to class after lunch the teacher naturally wanted to know why he was late. A very excited Lucien whispered to Toni, the teacher, that he had been watching five Americans walking down the road.

Marie-Antoinette Piriou, "Toni," was our first contact with a member of the third level of the Resistance. She knew who belonged to the active Resistance. She immediately turned her class over to another teacher and came looking for us.

In the meantime we were intercepted by a Frenchman who had been wounded in the leg by the Germans in 1940. Mr. Dorlot found it incredible that the five of us were boldly marching down the road in broad daylight. He suggested rather forcefully that we get off the road and follow him. He led us to a small village about two kilometers away and had us go into the basement of a small bistro where we were served a lunch of roast beef and a pot au feu, in addition to three bottles of red wine.

After consuming "beaucoup de" hot soup and several glasses of red wine we had forgotten that there was a war on and that we were in a tight situation. The five or six French men and women who were with us in the bistro seemed no more than us to be worried about the war at that moment. And they seemed as happy to have us with them as we were to find ourselves there.

By mid-afternoon Toni, the Plouray schoolteacher, found us soaking up the sun in the tall grass about a hundred meters from the bistro. With great emotion Toni assured us that she would get us back to England as she had done for other American pilots a year earlier. She advised us to stay in this open field until after dark, when she would return for us.

At 6PM Toni, followed by six French men and women, returned to our hiding place and led us over a number of "petits chemins" (small dirt paths. Trans.) a distance of two kilometers to the schoolhouse in Plouray.

Our group of five Americans stayed in the Plouray schoolhouse for five weeks, a most difficult time for all concerned. Providing food for five hungry young men was not easy and it became almost the principal activity of the community. The school children brought their teacher butter, eggs, and bread. The local butcher supplied meat, the baker bread, and every visitor brought cider or wine.

We had visitors every evening, including Mr. Veley, the mayor; Miss Louisette, the town telegraph operator who assured the Gestapo that the town had never seen an American airman; Mr. Letolguenec, the notary; Mr. Lhéridaud, the district inspector of schools; Mr. Machadoo, the butcher; and finally Mr. Pailly, owner of the only hotel in town. We suspected that all the children in Toni's class knew that we were hiding in the schoolhouse.

Joséphine Veley and her fiancé Marcel Pasco, both of whom lived with their parents very near the school, shared with Toni the responsibility of taking care of us.

During our fifth week at the Plouray school, it was decided that we would go to speak with the leaders of the local Resistance and seek another hiding place. Mr. Lhéridaud drove Toni and me ten kilometers to the town of Gourin where we met the mayor, Mr. Kergaravat. He immediately grasped the seriousness of the situation and ordered us to split up and, moreover, that we be moved immediately.

Lt. King and I were sent to a small bistro about four kilometers from Plouray where we spent two weeks with Jean Violo, his wife Francine, and his two sisters Yvonne and Marie.

Two weeks later we were moved to the Tournebride hotel, where we stayed in a third-floor apartment with Mr. and Mrs. Antoine Garnier, whose home had been destroyed during one of the many bombings of Lorient and who now were living in the hotel operated by their nephew, Joseph Goulian, and his wife Alice.

After two weeks in the hotel we were moved to the farm of Louis and Baptist Lanaor, who had been waiters at a resort near Grenoble but had returned to the family farm to avoid being sent to Germany for STO.

On the fourth day at the Lanaor farm Mr. Lecren and his two sons, René and Désiré, came in a truck from the town of Gourin to take us to the train station for the journey to Guingamp. On arrival at the station we were met by André Chareton, who led us to the home of Mr. and Mrs. Désiré Laurent, a local policeman and his wife. Their home was two blocks from German headquarters.

On the second evening François Kerumbran and George Lecun came to the Laurent house to listen to the BBC. When the 6 o'clock news broadcast said "Hello, to everyone at Alphonse's house," the Frenchmen knew that a motor gunboat had departed Dartmouth, England to pick up airmen on the northern coast of Brittany, near Plouha.

After a half-hour of bumps and turns in the small truck of François Kerumbrun we arrived at the house of Jean and Marie Gicquel, later known as the House of Alphonse. Twenty-five of us were briefed by "Captain Harrison of British Military Intelligence Service," actually Sgt. Major Lucien Dumais of the Canadian army, who had been parachuted into France to organize the Jedburgh network.

Present at the House of Alphonse were some of the members of the Jedburgh network—François LeCornac, Job Mainguy, Pierre Huet, Jean and Marie Gucquel, Maria-Thérèse LeCalvez, and Jean and Jeannette Trehiou. At midnight we departed La Maison d'Alphonse for a two-kilometer walk to the rendezvous with MGB 503 of the 5th Fleet of the British Royal Navy. After several anxious hours at sea we arrived safe and sound back in England. I had been in the hands of the French Resistance for sixty-two days.

Although I have told you my personal story, I today represent over nine hundred members of the Air Force Escape and Evasion

Society who have had similar experiences. Most of the leaders of the Jedburg network were recognized and decorated by American and British information services but hundreds of unknown French men and women who risked their lives to help us were not. It was dangerous to know names, so we did not ask.

Immediately after the war British and American authorities made a sincere effort to locate and recognize those men and women of France who helped Allied airmen, and for many years the Royal Air Force Escaping Society and the Air Forces Escape and Evasion Society have honored hundreds of "méconnus" (unknowns. Trans.) in England and in the United States.

The majority of the brave men and women of the French Resistance who risked their lives to help Allied airmen are deceased, but they are not forgotten by the airmen.

Nous n'oublierons jamais. (We will never forget. Trans.)

(Based on a translation by Roger Asselineau.)

Testimony of Étienne Lafond

Before the war I began my apprenticeship as a manufacturer of fabrics at Louviers in the factory founded by my maternal grandfather.

My uncle Charles Miquel took me as co-director and associate at the same time as his daughter Denise.

The production was integrated: it had dying, spinning, weaving, and dressing; it employed around 450 workers in a city of 9,000 inhabitants.

In 1943 my uncle accepted the task of establishing an "antenna" of the Alliance network, later nicknamed Noah's Ark. The day of his arrest, my cousin Denise, whose fate I was to share, denied everything she was accused of, as I myself did. To the SD officer who said to her, "You cannot deny at least that your father is 'Leopard' and you yourself are 'Mangouste'?" she replied: "But it's Noah's Ark!" The German replied to her, "You just baptized your movement."

My uncle was "Leopard," my cousin "Mangouste," I was the driver of the truck, René Lardeux was "Python," and the farmer who received the parachute drops, Robert Pezard, was "Ponnette II."

In this way an entire organization bent on being clandestine was put in place. Right in the middle of an operating factory! Visitors with suspicious looks circulated in it at odd hours. One evening I received "Cygogne," who left me a radio transmission set; I subsequently got to know two other radio operators, "Rossignol" and "Cyge."

The transmissions took place in certain storehouses of the factory, which gave rise at different times to the passing through of radio-detection trucks in the neighboring streets.

The parachute drops that took place on the Pezards' property in Fouqueville were brought back to the factory by a factory truck filled with bales of wool; since Fouqueville was approximately between Elbeuf and Louviers on the plateau of Neubourg, the itinerary of the truck was credible.

117

Once returned to the factory the truck had to be unloaded in unusual places and its load transported and hidden in wells and shafts that gave access to different arms of the river.

All the people who participated in this operation were not a network. They formed that unrecognized resistance in France, that "nebula" of the Resistance, without which the networks would not have been able to function.

All those who assisted with the parachute drops and all those who hid arms and mail were the dust of this nebula, like the overseer at the factory with the famous shafts, Émile Rouley, who was arrested, deported, and who died at Buchenwald.

My uncle, who was arrested, was liberated by mistake during the air attack on the prison at Évreux. He was hidden by the nebula, and he was clandestinely transported to Paris by this same nebula.

All the others were deported—my cousin to Ravensbruck, myself to Ellrich—Lardeux died at Ellrich. And the Pezards were also deported, one to Buchenwald, the other to Ravensbruck, where both died.

Thus no action would have been possible without the omnipresent existence of this nebula that extended far beyond the confines of the factory, because it encompassed all the families of the personnel, and more—perhaps some thousands of people.

All these people trusted, confided in, each other; they heard stories (which were crosschecked) about suspicious comings and goings, about unusual transports, about the more or less discreet surveillance of the Germans.

They took stock that bizarre things were happening. Did they approve? Perhaps not. Some rightly found us perhaps a bit "unserious," unaware of the danger we were running and that we placed others in.

Perhaps they thought that the future of the factory, their future, would be compromised if it lost its leadership....

Others silently encouraged us. But in all cases, everyone was quiet and surrounded us with an assured complicity.

All united against the detested occupier.

If we were betrayed it wasn't by them but by an English Nazi belonging to Mosley's party who had infiltrated the network in England and who was parachuted into France!

After my arrest my wife recovered the transmitter set that had been hidden within a fireplace. She put it in my sister Catherine's baby basket, put the baby in it on top of the transmitter, and took the set to a friend so that he could deposit it in the river that crossed his property. This friend did so, quite simply, despite the risk he ran. He didn't belong to any organization. He never spoke of it. He was part of the unrecognized resistance.

Testimony of Jean-Marie Breton

This is a testimony concerning certain actions of my father, Charles Breton.*

Charles Breton was a manufacturer and from 1941 to 1944 he was the mayor of Chateauneuf-la-Forêt in Haute-Vienne, named by Vichy.

1. At the request of an officer of the Army of the Armistice he hid twenty military vehicles in the sheds of the paper factory he controlled (under the straw).
2. In the village, as mayor he protected, among others, a Jewish dentist (under the false name of Clavin) and an escaped prisoner and doctor (Dr. Hamon).
3. From 1941 until his death in 1944 he participated in safeguarding the wealth of one of his clients, a Jewish businessman from Paris (Mr. Loëw).

---

* Please note: I limit my testimony to these three facts about which I have compared my memories as a child (nine to eleven years) with those of my brother (nineteen to twenty-one at the time).

Testimony of Mr. André Pertuzio

The Genesis and Unfolding of November 11, 1940

I am going to say a few words about November 11, 1940, about which Alain Griotteray has already spoken, in order to add a few small things and especially to answer the question: Why? Actually it is quite simple. At that time we were the children of combatants of the Great War and our childhood had been nursed on stories about it; we were proud of being French because France had been crowned with the honors of its victory in 1918. We were a great power and we thought that the French army was the first in the world.

We, alas, were undeceived in June 1940 and I have to say that for me, as for many others, that caused shame. Rapidly replaced, moreover, by the humiliation of the Occupation and by the anger of seeing gray and green uniforms in Paris.

How this demonstration began I do not know. I believe that among those who took part no one can say exactly what was the start and, above all, who were the organizers, because there weren't any. And that is precisely the particular character of this rather extraordinary event: it was spontaneous.

It started in the [university] faculties at the end of October-the beginning of November 1940. We learned by word of mouth, there had been tracts distributed, an "appeal" on the radio in London, and above all the announcement that at the request of the occupying authorities—more than a request too—it was forbidden to demonstrate and go to the tomb of the unknown soldier on November 11, 1940. At that time there were in all the [university] faculties—me, I was the president of the corpus of law at the time; we had contacts with people of letters, of sciences...—secret meetings, but not really organizations. In the high schools it was different. In fact, because the high schools were closed places they lent themselves a little better to an organization of the demonstration. But the students didn't

123

know at all who would go to the Arc de Triomphe, with the exception of friends we knew. Those at the high schools didn't know that the college students were going to demonstrate and vice versa.

We set a rendezvous for 3:30PM in front of the Arc de Triomphe. The high school students, especially those of Janson-de-Sailly, went to lay down their flowers under the eyes of dumbfounded police who allowed them to proceed...but not for a long time.

When the great "battalions" of the other Parisian high schools and of the faculties arrived the Germans intervened and they started, of course, to push back and disperse the demonstrators. I will pass by the rather great confusion of the thing, but it was a serious affair: there were more than 2,000 demonstrators, perhaps more, I don't know, but it is certain that there were a thousand questionings, 120 to 130 arrests, and some of our friends were very seriously assaulted, especially in the prison of Cherche-Midi.

What conclusion to draw? One must be proud of the action of these young people. I do not say that because I was there. I was there completely by chance and I certainly didn't have the impression of "resisting" and certainly not of being a hero.

We knew nothing of how this was going to go off. The only thing we could hope for was that November 11 wouldn't be politically co-opted. And of course there were efforts in that direction. For example, that November 11, 1940 was organized by Communist youth. So we must recall the truth.

This demonstration was totally apolitical. It wasn't a question of protesting against anything whatsoever but the occupier. It was a spontaneous patriotic demonstration. That is the truth.

Testimony of Mr. Asselineau

Aid to Allied Pilots

Frankly, I have only a few things to add to what Mr. Ralph Patton said. In 1944 I belonged to an escape and evasion network. At the time I was a teacher at the Carnot high school in Paris. I had female colleagues in the north of France who would bring to Paris pilots downed throughout the region. My task was to find shelters for them before their departure to Brittany. I had to take them on the Metro, have them take the train to Brittany, and then sometimes, because they would get bored, take them out for a while.

I remember a particularly exhilarating day in the spring of 1944 when, with a colleague, we had taken out two American pilots as far as the Trocadero. It was a Sunday and many German soldiers were strolling there. We had the profound joy of contemplating Paris before us, the Paris that had made Hitler dance for joy a few months earlier. Thus at times like this there were recompenses for the work we were doing.

The pilots that we guided were often very conscious of the dangers that we were running. Some would say, "Me, if I am recaptured, I will be treated as a prisoner of war, but you, you will be doubtlessly be condemned to death." In fact that is what happened to me personally.

In truth, though, all the Allied pilots were not treated in the simple way that they thought they would be. When I was a prisoner at Fresnes I had in my cell for a while an American officer and pilot downed in the Bordeaux region. He had been badly treated; they had taken his identity card. He had found a way of escaping. He was recaptured, following a betrayal no doubt. They had kept him for several weeks in very insalubrious places. Even though he was a rather vigorous man—he had been a lifeguard in Florida—he had contracted bronchitis. In my cell he suffered terribly from asthma. I was sometimes obliged to call the guard in order to ask that the doctor on call would come to attend to him during his emergencies.

He was interrogated by a German officer of the Luftwaffe who was very surprised that he had been treated that way. And it is very likely that he was not treated liked a prisoner of war after all that he had tried. He probably was sent to some extermination camp. I never heard any news about him. I pointed out his case as soon as the Allies arrived in Paris. Later in the United States I wrote to the Pentagon. No one ever responded to me. I fear very much that he disappeared.

Testimony of Robert Richard

The Resistance in Loir-et-Cher: The Prosper Network[1]

I belong to the Voluntary Combatants of the Resistance. My resistance took place in Loir-et-Cher. Before developing what I have to say, I would like to read the last paragraph of the editorial of Mr. Couffrant, to whom tribute was rendered at the Invalides two months ago in October (he died in July). His editorial is in the February issue of the *Fondation de la Résistance* and says this: "[T]hird risk, finally: that the agents or witnesses tell tall tales sixty years afterwards is excusable, but still prejudicial to the historical truth. For all our comrades who died in combat or in the camps we ought to take care that the Resistance is truthfully represented to future generations. In this lies the importance and the difficulty of the work of the historian. Historical and pedagogical consensus, the common points of reference that unite historians known for the quality of their work, ought to aid us in maintaining historical vigilance and in speaking the truth when falsification becomes too flagrant."

I would like also to read the letter that I addressed to Mr. Matteoli, dated February 22, 2000: "Mr. President, with the agreement of several individuals belonging to the directing committee of the National Confederation of Voluntary Combatants of the Resistance (CNCVR), which held a meeting at Grasse from October 1-4, 1999, I was instructed to develop a subject, June 21, 1943—which I had only touched on in Dijon in September 1998—which was the date of the arrests at Sologne and the beginning of the disaster of the Prosper network. The report of my intervention is part of the documents that I sent to the Foundation of the Resistance November 15 last. Allow me to ask you to use your eminent authority to help me make known to the future generations an episode of the Second World War that has been totally hidden for more than a half century

127

for reasons that ought not to prevail today. Soon there will be no more survivors among those who participated—often unwittingly—in the dramatic events that had been planned with the wholly understandable and justified design of contributing to the landing and final victory."

As I said to the eminent members of the directing committee of the CNCVR, it was in 1984, and thus forty-one years after these events, that I got to know Mr. Couffrant. I first met him, however, at the beginning of June 1943 when he, accompanied by a couple, Pierre and Jacqueline (no last name given. Trans.), had paid a visit to us, an embryonic underground constituted by a group of eight réfractaires from the STO.

During a visit to his home at Romorantin in 1988 I learned what had been his itinerary: arrested at dawn June 21, 1943 with his team while returning from a parachute drop, internment at Blois, then transfer to Fresnes, then deportation to Mauthausen at the beginning of November 1943.

At his return to France in May 1945 he received a cold welcome at the Hôtel des Invalides because he had served under a foreign flag. Having myself had the luck of passing through all these vicissitudes without any damage, I made the decision to devote myself entirely to the official rehabilitation of these first resisters who were ignored and sometimes treated ignominiously by those that a famous politician called "resisters of August 32, 1944."

In 1991 a monument consecrated to the memory of the Special Operations Executive (SOE) agents of section F killed in combat or who died during deportation was dedicated at Valençay in the presence of Her Majesty, the Queen Mother of England. They were agents specially trained in England, operating under British control, and conducting sabotage on French territory with the help of locals, many of whom were arrested.

In England the heroism of the Prosper network earned it the posthumous decoration of the DSO. Could not France posthumously award a very small number of medals of the Resistance to those who were true resisters, active from the beginning, who gave their lives for the success of the landing or who, upon their return from deportation, had to suffer indifference and sometimes the hostility of the authorities in place and even in certain cases appear before tribunals in order to defend their honor before a profoundly misinformed public opinion?

It would especially be a case of posthumously honoring the memory of Pierre Culioli (1912-1994), founder of the Adolphe network, and Roger Couffrant (1910-1996), a leader of the Adolphe network, the group at Romorantin. Confronted with proof collected by the German SD, who were kept abreast of their activities by the double agent Derricourt, both were obliged at the time of their arrest, June 21, 1943, to hand over an important part of the arms parachuted in since September 1942. Incarcerated at Fresnes, then (Roger Couffrant) deported to Mauthausen in November 1943, and Buchenwald (Pierre Culioli) in August 1944, on their return they had to answer for their acts before the law. Even though recognized as not guilty, they remained scarred for life by hardships not suffered by, and the suspicions of, a population totally ignorant of the dramatic circumstances of their arrest.

Response of Professor François-Georges Dreyfus

I would like to respond to Mr. Richard. First of all, in the *Histoire de la Résistance* that I wrote, the case of the Prosper network, with its reasons and dramatic consequences, was examined. And secondly, I never neglected the role of the SOE in my own book.

Response of Jean-Jacques de Bresson, National President of the Decorated of the Resistance

I would like to respond to the suggestion to reopen the time limit for the awarding of medals of the Resistance. I would like to say two things. The first, the medal of the Resistance can be given posthumously, following a procedure that is rather complex but does exist, on the condition that it be awarded to people who were killed during the war.

Other than that, the awarding of the medal of the Resistance ended in March 1947 and I do not at all believe that it would be possible to reopen this particular time limit. Decorations, we know, were given with a certain amount of arbitrariness, that is true. Everyone knows this, including the decorated, but the value of a decoration such as the medal of the Resistance lies precisely in that it was only granted during the war or immediately afterwards, beginning with its creation. As everyone knows, that was done by General de Gaulle in London, February 9, 1943.

Note

1.   One could complete the testimony of R. Richard with the work of Richard Seiler, *La tragédie du Réseau Prosper* (Paris, Pygmalion, 2003) (note of F-G Dreyfus).

Testimony of Alain Jurian

In 1944 I was ten years old and lived through all the events in Ain of which you spoke. My father belonged to a group of resisters of the underground of Ain, commanded by Petit. Three years ago I felt the need to rediscover what my father had done.

I had the unexpected luck of finding a woman, Mrs. Di Carlo, who is an historian and who has written an extraordinary history of the entire region. I also had the joy of rediscovering Mr. Thorossian, who was in my father's group and then left with the army of the Alps. On behalf of my generation I would like to say to them, and to you, thank you.

Testimony of Mrs. Jacqueline Di Carlo

I published a book in 1994 that relates certain episodes of the war that took place in a canton of the district of Ain, the canton of Saint-Rambert-en-Bugey. For the book I interviewed a large number of participants, including thirty members of the underground, and I had in hand documents that were written at the time of the events. It is these accounts that I would like to tell you about today because they perfectly illustrate that "unrecognized resistance" that then existed.

A quick sketch of the region: Lyon is to the west, Genève to the east, Mâcon to the north, Grenoble to the south. The Cluze des hôpitaux is an important passageway, because it's through it that National Route 504 leads toward Savoy, Italy and Switzerland. I will speak first about the director of a textile factory, Mr. André Huet. No one ever knew the role he played during this period. It was on the occasion of the appearance of my book in 1994 that he wrote his memoirs and hence that we learned about him. He was the king of forgers. From 1942 on, with the help of doctors, secretaries of the mayoralty, and mayors he created false dossiers in order to allow certain prisoners of war to return. They were returned for the sake of their families and the ailing. He was also aided in this by the judge of the canton, who one night told him that the number of false dossiers created by him would incur for him at the minimum 135 years of hard labor.

This network of forgers continued to operate when young people refusing to report for the STO had to go to other communes. This factory director had an easy enough role, because he employed people from elsewhere and sent others to work in factories of the same group. He had relations with many different people. One day he was surprised to see arrive a box containing fifty rubber stamps. They were from mayoralties that had been bombed and whose archives were completely destroyed. Thus no verification was possible. This box of rubber stamps later went to Commander Henri Petit, according to Roman Petit.

Then there was the famous law concerning obligatory service in Germany (the STO). I interviewed people who had been called and I was struck by the fact that some of them said to me: "I was alone, I didn't know what to do, I had gone to my friends who told me that I had to obey. One is obliged." This person, however, didn't want to go. She tried to find some peasants who would take her in, in exchange for her working. In the town next to it, the young people there were stronger because they were more numerous; they had four or five. They were aided by an escape chain that passed through a horticulturist of Ambérieu (who had an uncle in the country) and café operators of Saint-Rambert. All these people organized themselves in order to send these young people to the country folk who wanted to take them in or, if not, to the woodcutting operations that were quite numerous in the region.

Others sought ways to preserve themselves so that they could go join de Gaulle. A group of fifteen set off for Switzerland. Unfortunately when they arrived in May 1943 Switzerland had closed its borders. They were obliged therefore to return. When they returned they were told they had to go to Germany.

With the danger getting more definite the Resistance attempted to organize. And one can say that in our neck of the woods the organization of the Resistance was the work of Captain Henri Petit. He was the commander of the base at Cannes at the time of the Armistice in 1940. He threw himself into resistance from the beginning and in 1941 was part of the Espoir network.

Another incident: A dozen people took the road to Spain. They went to Lourdes. After crossing the border they were naturally arrested on the other side. After having spent six months in Spanish jails they arrived in Casablanca where they joined the army of Africa. This was in November, while they had left in May.

During this time the Roman Petit network was organized. The most difficult thing was to supply the needs of all the young people who were more and more numerous. Therefore in the town a clandestine committee of support was created, charged with bringing them both natural goods and cash.

When a peasant offered an isolated barn in the mountains the PC was founded. There were twenty under the orders of Petit and, as I said, the main problem was finding food. One of these underground members, Hubert Mermet of Saint-Rambert, was called "the Superintendent" because he was charged with finding food. He rode on bicycle throughout all the country roads, his sack on his back. He had his regular providers, peasants who gave him lard and potatoes, and a butcher, Mr. Turc, who tried to steal and set aside everything he could. Finally the group became too large and it split in two, then took in all sorts of people: Poles, Yugoslavs, Spanish Republicans, also Jews.

I would like to add one thing in ending. In the district of Ain we are trying to produce a CD-Rom capturing and conveying all these deeds of resistance for those attending high school and college or university.

Testimony of José Bellec

First point: Mr. de Bresson responded a moment ago to Mr. Richard; I would just add that there are not more than 2,200 to 2,300 known holders of the Medal of the Resistance.

Second point: I would like to address myself especially to historians. A few days ago I participated in a colloquium of this genre entitled "Resistance, Community, and Reconstruction." I had the task of speaking of the officials under the occupation. I noticed that there was a snare that historians need to avoid.

I was given a considerable (750 pp.) volume by a historian, drawn from a dissertation and well documented from the archives. For this historian officials were rather insignificant, with the exception of a few rare personages who proved their courage and heroism, thus saving the honor of the Resistance.

But that is to forget what it was to write a memorandum under the Occupation and under the eyes of the Germans, the SS, and to forget all that we knew. It is true: I myself refused to be the cabinet head for the Lemoine prefecture, the regional prefecture of Marseille. But let there be no misunderstanding: I do not accuse the prefectural body of collaborating.

I would like to convey to you some recently discovered truths. In the French police—so often spoken ill of, by generalizing—there were eight hundred and sixty-seven who died on the field of honor, six hundred and thirty as members of the national security force and the rest for the prefecture of police. I have the official list. Most of the time these have remained unknown. On another hand, do you know that Marie-Madeleine Fourcade in 1965 wrote that in her network she enlisted one hundred and thirty-four resisters, from the commissioner of police to the guardian of the peace?

José Bellec is national vice president of the Decorated of the Resistance and vice president of the Federation of the Deported of the Resistance.

Yet again, Édouard Edmond Michelet, one of the most emblematic members of the Resistance, wrote the following: "without the collaboration of these often discreet officials, whose action could never display itself spectacularly as with the liberation of Paris, well, the Resistance would have been hobbled, strangled, and it could not have existed."

I would like to report another thing unknown or ignored by the historians, something we discovered and verified last year. In the prefectural corps of the Occupation, among the prefects, sub-prefects, secretary-generals of the prefecture, and cabinet heads, there were one hundred and sixty-four medal award winners of the Resistance. That appeared to us to be an enormous number. But it is a fact, it has been verified.

I therefore draw the attention of historians to the necessity, as long as there are still living witnesses, to have recourse to these witnesses and to consult their archives. Now, the historian to whom I alluded above, while he doesn't plume himself on this, says that his research is based on "the archives" and very little on testimonies. That is a mistake.

Testimony of Jeannette Schlagdenhauffen, Who Resisted with the Catholic Group of the Sorbonne

Whether it was in my family or with the Ursuline Sisters of Vannes where I was raised, I was always taught to love France and never to resign myself to the German Occupation. Very quickly, in my philosophy class the last wonderful letter of d'Estienne d'Orves to his wife was circulated, the one written before he was shot with his comrades.

All those who surrounded me, whatever their opinions, suffered so much in their hearts from the Occupation that none of them was capable of being pro-German. Doubtlessly, there were BOFs[1] and women you no longer spoke to because they had succumbed to the seduction of some of the men in green and gray.

Personally, I had the good fortune to be the assistant scout leader of Marianne de Charrette, who was thrown in prison with her sister Geneviève because she did not submit to the advances of the German officers living on her father's property. I also had the luck of having as a classmate Isabelle Renault and as a professor of psychology her sister Jacqueline, today the Prioress General of the Dominicans of the Holy Spirit, both sisters of Colonel Rémy whose entire family was arrested and imprisoned in Fresnes.

This background is enough to explain my adherence in the autumn of 1943 to the Resisters of the Catholic Group at the Sorbonne. I wasn't doing much there besides distributing the publication *Temoignage chrétien*, until the day I was asked to go retrieve at the house of Jean-Pierre Baraduc, arrested at one in the morning, a machinegun and some grenades. At that time it was said that girls risked less than the guys.

With Viviane Jamati I rang at the house on the rue de Rennes. Mrs. Baraduc opened the door for us (the Gestapo had just left) and, very emotional, she told us that it seemed to her that the Germans had not taken anything with them and that her son, the president of the Confederation of Saint-Vincent-de-Paul of the arrondissement, could not have done anything wrong.

We were allowed to enter into the room of the young man where the Germans had turned everything upside-down. And as inconceivable as the thing was, we found in a hosiery drawer two big blue packages, tightly tied. One, relatively light, contained a statue of the Virgin Mary; the other, much heavier, we opened. It was a taken-apart machinegun! But there were no grenades. I do not know how the story ended, since I never saw one or the other again. As for the machinegun which we carried on the metro in the midst of the Germans, we deposited it in the cellars of the Sorbonne.

A few days after the landing, under the name of Jacqueline, with a knapsack and on bicycle, I was assigned to go to Neuf-le-Chateau and Jouy-en-Josas. I met Dominique, a medical inspector after the Resistance, who taught me (and Charlotte) how to code the messages of the northern delegation of General de Gaulle. Each morning, coming from Paris, Lucien, who was a concierge at rue Vaneau, would bring us precious envelops and we would give him the telegrams received the night before from various agents who were in contact with the radio transmitters who worked during the night.

We rode a lot on the roads around our residence because the places fixed on the map for rendezvous covered ten kilometers in each direction. Protected by the generous Mr. Milliès, an important proprietor in the area, whose son had a leg amputated because he had stepped on a mine, we were assured of having milk each day. We had few, but good, contacts with the neighborhood. We never observed anything shocking, but we did experience a great joy when the Americans arrived.

One day Lucien, sporting an armband of the Wermarcht, helped us cross the German roadblocks without any damage to our bicycles; we were wholly taken by the sight of soldiers in disarray, whom we with great joy saw leave. With some trouble we arrived in Paris and it was at Mrs. de Saint-Phalle's on rue Seguier that we continued to code messages, some of which went to Montparnasse and to General Leclerc. It is impossible to describe or convey the emotion we felt—we and all the people of Paris—when all the bell towers of all the churches of the capital began to ring.

Paris was liberated but the war continued. Besides a tiny minority who out of anti-Communism chose to fight on the Eastern front and a few base profiteers, the French unanimously were against the occupier.

But I also owe it to historical truth to say that in Cantal from 1943 on my husband's Alsatian family was hidden in an isolated farm whose owner was none other than the local president of the Legion of Combatants created by Marshal Petain, and no one ever gave them away. Today again, I thank from the bottom of my heart those French whose love of France was the sole motive of their actions.

Note

1.   BOF, "Beurre, Oeufs, Frommages" (Butter, Eggs, Cheese), the abbreviation for those who profited from the occupation.

Testimony of Colette Gerbaud

In October 1940 my mother opened the door of our apartment in Paris and saw a French policeman who had come looking for "Mr. Gerbaud, who is Jewish." My mother answered, "It is not my husband who is Jewish but me." The policeman answered her, "Then he will have to wait for the Jerry!" And he left.

I have often thought of this policeman who saved my mother's life and I've always regretted not being able to thank him, him or his descendants, for the happiness of having my mother alive and at home during that period.

My mother was originally from the Jewish community of Alsace. My grandfather wanted to remain in France (in 1885, when my mother was born, Alsace was German) so he came to Paris with his nine children in 1893. The family was poor but patriotic. My mother enlisted in 1914 as a volunteer nurse and served during the entire war (first sent to Châteauroux, she was subsequently named head nurse at the hospital of Montargis. She received a medal for her tireless devotion at the time of the Spanish flu epidemic.). My mother was a remarkable woman, endowed with indomitable courage. She always refused to wear the yellow star, and she braved all dangers, for example, by several times going to save what she could from the apartment of one of her brothers who was then in the non-occupied zone. She found herself in terrible situations, but never experiencing fear she dominated and overcame all of them. Her Jewish family remaining in Alsace was taken away by the Germans and died in the concentration camps.

My father, although educated by the Brothers at Christian schools, had rather latitudinous views on religion. There never were problems concerning religion at home and my brother, unlike me, converted to Catholicism and even became a "traditionalist." My father was very talented; he also was very good and willing to help. He spent nights making false papers in order to save Jewish friends who wanted to escape to the New World. Moreover, he risked his life by putting in his name a place on rue Sorbier where our shoe-maker, a Jew from Central Europe, was hiding. On several occa-sions he helped in this way people he knew, at a time when that could get you executed.

In my mother's family a niece entered the Resistance. She was arrested one day and tortured on the rue des Saussaies. One of her sisters as well and her husband were also in the Resistance. A sister-in-law was a "mail box" for the Resistance. She told me how one day the Germans came to her house. She knew how to skillfully answer their questions and thus saved her life.

As for myself, I always carried the Cross of Lorraine on me at the period and I flouted the Germans. At school one of my friends, a Jewess of fifteen years old, had seen her parents led away by the Germans. She remained alone in the world. Her anti-Semitic house-keeper harassed her because she often returned home late, after the curfew. She was a resister. She distributed tracts just about every-where in buildings. One day I no longer saw her at school. I suppose that she perished, like her parents, in the camps. I believe they were Jews from Poland.

One of my history teachers had lost his eighteen-year-old son, who was active in the Resistance. Young men of twenty-two in my quarter gave their lives to defend Paris in 1944. A monument recalls their sacrifice in Maurice Gardette square. They were "Émile de Gorter, André Mansuy, and their heroic companions fallen for France, Au-gust 20, 1944."

A friend from Rosny-sous-Bois told me one day that he had been forcibly sent to the STO in Germany. He, however, decided on his own to get to England via Morocco. He therefore found himself in Marseille, waiting for a ship, in 1942. Since the non-occupied zone had been taken over by the Germans he couldn't depart, and he was picked up by the Germans again, who once more sent him to Ger-many. There, working hard in a butcher shop when he could he gave his bread to the French prisoners in the neighboring camp. That caused him to be tried and severely punished. He spent seven months in prison in Germany and did not return to France until after the hostilities. He was emaciated and very sick. He told me that he had attempted to leave for England, "like all the young people of my age." Such were the youth of the 1940s!

Testimony of Louise Balfet

My Resistance at Eighteen

I was for some years, in fact from December 1940 until the Liberation, a liaison agent of one of my aunts. I never would have related this period of my youth if friendly solicitations had not made me, in particular those of the Air Forces Escape and Evasion Society, of which I am proud to be a life member. I therefore will make my modest contribution to "the duty of remembering" and, even more simply, to a chapter of our Resistance, one I conducted "in the family." Here are a few of my memories that were lying dormant in my mind. They will allow the inspiration of one of the principal networks of escape and evasion to Spain, especially of American pilots, to come to life, if only fleetingly.

My Aunt: At the School of Mata Hari

A very uncommon woman was Marthe Putman, my father's sister-in-law, who became Lil Vanwijhe after her divorce from my uncle Charles Delrue. For a long time she was kept away from the family, since we were a bourgeois family that her seedy past made shudder. For imagine, during the Great War as an agent of the Second Bureau she had established relations with Mata Hari and had succeeded, conveyed by a submarine no less, in taking photographs of a German base! After the divorce she married a reputable Dutch doctor. Officially becoming a painter, she chose for her husband's retreat an area with a dry climate: Capendu, an agreeable borough of Aude, on the route from Carcassonne to Narbonne. There in 1938 she bought the château du Parc. The Jewish origins of her husband must have dictated this unexpected choice far from the German border.... I do not know the circumstances in which she reconnected with her ex-brother-in-law, my father. Having long-time business connections

145

in Mazamet, he had chosen to repair there at the time of the exodus. Despite these circumstances, with the joy and insouciance of an eighteen year old I discovered these lands in the South.

And I was happy to be invited for the very first time to Capendu for Christmas 1940 by this unknown aunt.

My Christmas Night 1940: Entry into Service!

Cars lacking motor fuel being stored in the garage, it was necessary to travel by train to go from Mazamet to Capendu. An expedition!

I have no memory of the arrival of my parents at the station in Capendu. But I, not being able to make my own way out of my packed compartment, I was pressed out on the wrong side of the train and on the wrong side of a partition. Thus it came about that I was presented to my aunt black with smoke and sweat. I found a small woman not lacking in allure, whose penetrating and authoritative look pierced through me. She rather shocked me (as she would continue to do, in other regards) by the eccentricity of her apparel and her red hair. It would be difficult to pass unnoticed looking like this in Capendu in 1940.

I emphasize the date: it was December 24, 1940, at night. Christmas Eve, a holiday, despite everything. We were at table. Someone rang. The Dutch majordomo (my aunt had a majordomo!) told Madame that someone was waiting at the entrance. She quite simply told us that it was a fugitive Dutchman that she had to help, by hiding him and organizing his passage to Spain. She added, also quite simply, that she would need my help, with a tone that indicated she would not tolerate any discussion.

In this way I rather proudly discovered that while I was preparing my baccalaureate at the high school for young ladies at Castres, an organization for resisting Germany existed—and in my family!—a family that had been Gaullist since his "appeal" June 18, 1940. My aunt had sensed (unless she was already informed) the perfect agreement that existed on this point between the convictions of my parents and her activities. In this way I found myself by chance a modest link of an escape and evasion network, as modest as it was unexpected on my part.

My Action at Capendu

After this initiation, having returned to Mazamet I received several calls. My aunt, always smiling and at ease, said to me, "I need you as you are young and athletic." And I left right away.

Since I left without my parents, it was needless to take the long train ride again. To get to Capendu from Mazamet I got on my bicycle, crossed the Black Mountain, and three hours later I arrived dead tired but happy at my aunt's château. Each time I spent several days with her: officially it was a holiday. I fished in Aude. I gathered grapes. I took part in the life of the village. Secondarily, if I can put it that way, my aunt would give me a message to deliver to such-and-such a recipient at Carcassonne, Narbonne, or Toulouse. I would not know either the military grade or the civilian status of the recipient. For these liaisons I took the train or a bicycle, or both. I often encountered difficulties in meeting my interlocutors. In fact, my profile as a big blonde and my northern accent, which often served me well with the Germans, made me rather suspicious on first meeting in the South. I passed for a foreigner, perhaps even a German!

At this point I would like to relate an anecdote. I was to convey a message to Toulouse to someone rather poetically named Dante, George Dante, of whom I only knew that he was a medical resident. Two days of trying availed nothing, no doubt because of my looks: he wasn't there, no one had seen him, he had left. I ended by abandoning the search for this mythical being. Later, though, I was charged with finding him just after he had escaped a trap. In order to be recognized I held one of my aunt's dogs in my arms (happily the dog was gentle). When the train stopped in the station at Capendu, to my great surprise I saw Gabriel Nahas—alias Dante—get off; I had known him in Mazamet where he—so young and already brilliant—gave lectures in the cadre of the FEDE (Federation of Protestant students). "It was you!" It was he. I forget how much time he remained hidden at my aunt's. I don't know anything about their common activities. I learned since that he had important responsibilities in the Françoise network based in Toulouse. Francoise, old before her time and in shaky health, ran a little business on rue Saint-Antoine du T. From it she ran this network, about which others have written the history and that earned her being decorated by General de Gaulle after the war. (Gabriel Nahas, who became an eminent pharmacologist, a professor at Columbia University, and a UN expert in the area of drugs, recounted part of his adventures in his book, *La filière du rail*.)

From time to time I performed different missions, simple liaisons, for this network and to help Gabriel Nahas. He worked not only with my aunt but also with another very active woman of Toulouse, Simone Calmes. During the entire war she hid, without her father knowing, fugitives in the loft of the family house, rue Raymond IV: Jews, réfractaires, escapees, etc.

Sometimes I traveled with the doctor of the village, the only person (along with his wife) who helped my aunt. Because of his profession, he was not inhibited by the poor availability of gasoline. We filled up from an official reservoir. And under the passenger seat, along with high-octane wine from friendly farms, messages were delivered.

Starting in November 1942 American pilots followed the Jews, Dutchmen, and réfractaires, [who had been aided] since the beginning of the war. They were, on average, four or five years older than I. In the heat and excitement of those days of clandestine life, of urgent actions, fear of betrayal, and the organization of decoys, an apparent insouciance covered a mad excitement on my part. I didn't become aware of the proximity of our ages except when, forty years later, their association, the AFEES, organized a trip to France and we reacquainted ourselves. What emotion! At the reception in Tarn organized by Gabriel Nahas, what then struck me, *then*, was that the planes that seemed so extraordinary to me at the time had been entrusted to such young men.

In the meantime, the South had been in its turn occupied by the German troops. The château at Capendu was progressively taken over: first by the office of a military dentist, then it was used as general quarters. The officers' food was prepared in the large château kitchen. We retained the use of the dining room. In attendance some nights were parachuted-in, escaped, and fleeing men! I had no fear, confident of the presence of mind and authority of my aunt. She told me, "No one will ever come here to look!" One night a German officer asked (he had seen me in the hallway) if he could come to listen to the radio in the living room. My aunt responded, "With pleasure, but we only listen to British radio." I remember his response: "That's no problem, it's only lies anyway." Must I then describe the stupefaction of the officer when he discovered on the living room table a German edition of *Mein Kampf*? And her saying, "You have read it? I read it in the original." Did he salute her and say "Heil Hitler"? I no longer remember, but I enjoyed that moment and I admired even more the sang-froid of my aunt.

Specific Operations

Two operations, one real, the other planned, still merit being recounted.

My cousin, the product of my aunt's first marriage, took part in her activities. He served as a relay in the channel to Spain. He was charged with bringing from Spain to France a microfilm hidden in a fingernail polishing brush, his only luggage! It was crazy to cross the border in the deep of winter, 1943, in the Spain-to-France direction. He was abandoned by his guide (who left after having secured his fee), he had to walk hours in the snow in his city clothes; he fell into a crevasse and fractured a vertebra. Nonetheless he was able to reach Elne, where he was taken in by a family that hid him in a barn. How my aunt learned about him I do not know, but she charged me with going to retrieve him. It was two days of travel, wrapped in special clothes reinforced by newspapers, and with a flask of high proof clandestine alcohol in my pocket. I had to sleep alone and locked in the unheated station at Lezignan, waiting for the morning train. I remember that for my breakfast (and merely to warm me up, since I wasn't lacking in courage) I drank deeply from the flask containing the powerful potion called 3/6. When I arrived at Elne, I had many difficulties in finding my cousin, going from house to house to find him. No one had heard of him. My perseverance—and my insistence—finally moved some nice people and I was able to reconnect with my exhausted and very ill cousin, who crushed me beneath his full weight as we sat together on the train. He showed me the brush that I would have to protect in case of trouble. I never knew its exact contents until after the war. To complete the story: My cousin used our network (the Dutch-Paris network) in the reverse direction to go to Switzerland, where he stayed six months wearing a corset.

The other episode in whose preparation I was modestly involved was more fantastic. The secret services, which were in regular contact with my aunt, had told her that in August 1944, Marshal von Rundstedt would make a stop at the château. His kidnapping was then planned for one night. But the marshal didn't stop as forecast.

Do I have to say that we felt the German collapse dawn? With an immense joy we saw the German convoys return from the west to the east, toward the Rhône valley. We said to ourselves, "We have won." We had awaited this moment since that Christmas night, 1940, when I had been unexpectedly initiated into these secret battles. Despite my timidity, I followed in the footsteps of my aunt fearlessly and joyfully.

In these few lines I wanted to render homage to that rather exceptional personage who lived a double life for four years. She was always at the mercy of being betrayed, but she interacted with everyone—the people of the village, the German officers, and, above all, with me—with the same ease. She thus pursued a most altruistic and rather efficacious work. As a result, I could truly say with her that last summer of the war in 1944: "We have won!"

Testimony of General Yves de Lauzières

Formerly, and not too long ago at that, the recalling of historical facts tended to be part of the apprenticeship in, and give a taste for, human greatness and dignity. Now, at the end of the century and of the millennium, it seems that recounting history means denying the values it claims to reveal and to cast doubt on everything. This colloquium is therefore quite welcome because the fresco of the Resistance is little known, it is misunderstood, and it is often denigrated.

What is said about it is sometimes merely a caricature. Moreover, it often lacks the essentials, so much is it encumbered with anecdotes that hide rather than reveal the history of the Resistance. That history ought to be impregnated with the ambiance that was the essence of everything and whose keystone was the German presence. Germany, Nazi or not, was for historical reasons the object of French antipathy for over one hundred years. And now Germany was here. It was the enemy against whom we had declared war and who, now, was among us, against our will, thinking he was at home.

It was Henri Frenay who said: "To know that there are Germans is one thing. To see them every day, is another." As long as one doesn't have this ambiance in mind, one distorts every explanation and every worthwhile understanding of the Resistance, because it was a constant presence for the Resistance.

Next, one must acknowledge that the Resistance was born from nothing. No school of thought ever imagined it, and even less taught it. Nonetheless, it succeeded—in only three and a half years—to grow in power, to expand, to grow in number and abilities, and to become an organization that the enemy could not neglect and with which it must come to terms. It is obvious that all this would often create incoherences and conflicts, both in ideas and in actions.

"But if we were neophytes, amateurs, nonetheless we weren't idiots" (Germaine Tillon). That is, despite the internal struggles and personal conflicts—which are undeniable but didn't constitute the

151

Resistance—despite the scrambling and the imperfections, it succeeded in "being."

It follows that for all these reasons the Resistance wasn't a civil war. A civil war is an armed struggle between two parts of the same country. Now General de Gaulle said: "The Resistance took all forms, but it was everywhere and always the same battle for the Fatherland."

One therefore cannot study the Resistance as one would a division or any organized corps of an army. That would be to believe that one is dealing with a normally constituted force, when it really was a mosaic of individuals (and "individualities"), having essentially the same common reference point—"the fight against the enemy"—but who were very disparate and lacked formal subordination to anyone, or among themselves.

In order to understand it therefore one must discover and grasp the specific reasoning informing its actions and activities. If not, one will describe a merely imaginary thing without real reference to the Resistance.

On such bases one can better understand the unrecognized resistance. For, if in a regular army on campaign there are soldiers whom one knows and others who are known, and there is established order and there are orders, in a resistance, on the other hand, there are active resisters dispersed and hidden among all the others and who act on their own initiative according to unprecedented norms. Now, "all the others" don't have any more sympathy for the Germans, whom they are forced to live and work alongside of. And how many of them took it upon themselves to run the greatest risks in order to aid and to help? Neither the former nor the latter knew better than anyone else how to go about things, or what was to be done. But instinctively they acted.

Do people talk about betrayals? Squealing on others? There were some, that's obvious, but how often, and with what effects? Let us not pontificate on this subject, which is more imagined than thoroughly known, for what was the real percentage of betrayers compared to the number of those who helped? Without any proof, some seek above all to devalue both the French and the Resistance.

It there had not been an unrecognized resistance we would not be here, because all of us benefited at one time or another, by act or omission (and the latter was sometimes worth the former). Without being exactly like "fish in water," we were at least all in the same boat. In particular I think of a train conductor who one day without me having said anything to him understood that I was in a spot of trouble and helped me extricate myself by taking me to an unguarded exit.

We have heard those of our generation criticize, lampoon, minimize, and ridicule both the Resistance movement and all our deeds. I therefore ask the generations to come to try to know and to understand what the Resistance was, truly, in the circumstances of the time. Then they will understand and acknowledge that it was not a "military parade," nor a diversion, that led thousands of Frenchmen and women into the networks, into the movements, into the undergrounds, on paths of escape outside France (there were some 23,000 escapees from France), and hundreds of thousands to form what we—here today—call "unrecognized resistance."

It is necessary therefore to distinguish between the histories and history, and to have the latter prevail over the former. In that way one will better understand and retain what the French who resisted truly were. The rest is fiction.

Testimony of R. J. Poujade

The Demonstration of August 25, 1940 at Quimper (Finistère)

Mr. President, Ladies and Gentlemen, it is a great honor to testify before you in this august space of the Republic.

I would like to specify that I was only one, among hundreds, in a spontaneous popular demonstration, one without an organizer, that took place August 25, 1940 at Quimper. I found myself by chance at one of the two places where the demonstration started, a demonstration against the traitors, the Breton separatists, then against the German occupiers.

I was twenty years old. I had fought in the 1939-1940 campaign, where I twice received citations. I had just escaped from a Frontstalaglazaret (a military hospital). Provided with false identity papers, I was leaving via Spain with a companion to rally the FFL. I therefore did not want to be noticed by the Germans, nor the police.

On August 25, 1940, the day commemorating Saint Louis, king of France—and four years later it will be that of the liberation of Paris—I found myself with some friends and former classmates at Quimper. We were chatting at the entrance of Place Saint-Corentin, which is between the cathedral and the mayoralty.

Around 10AM there was a crowd of parishioners around the cathedral, because one mass had finished and the main mass was about to begin. Suddenly a truck with German markings appeared, from which exited two civilians, their arms filled with newspapers, who went around the Place. One came toward our group. They waved *L'heure bretonne* and shouted out headlines. It was a pro-German publication. Forbidden by the prefecture, this weekly depended on the Propagandastaffel and the Abwehr.

R. J. Poujade is federal delegate of the FRRIC to the Committee of Action of the Resistance (CAR).

We knew that the Bishop of Quimper, who was rather strict but respected and a Breton, had firmly condemned at the end of July the agitations of the Breton separatists. He had had read in all the churches of Finistère a particularly clear and firm "warning" which, after referring to the Occupation and to the Breton traitors, ended by recalling the motto of Brittany: "Die rather than fail!"

Many of Quimper had also heard or read General de Gaulle's "appeal." I was among those who heard it. We also knew that the fishermen of the Isle of Sein had rallied to England. Minds therefore were not totally abandoned to the fantasies of the summer of 1940. We knew that those responsible for *L'heure brettone* had arrived in Quimper in vans marked with the WH of the Wehrmacht. But we didn't know that one of them, Olier Mordrel, would write later: "May 10, 1940, will remain in my memory as one of the great dates of my life. That morning the radio informed us that troops had passed the Belgian and Dutch borders: they opened for us the path of return...." That is clear.... This newspaper had announced Brittany's independence—under the authority of General Befelshaber of Rennes.

Mgr. Adolphe Duparc, the bishop of Quimper and of Leon, had been informed of the political intentions—in any event, they were openly stated—of the separatists and he had informed the prefects concerning their national-socialist character. One can say that his letter lit a match that only needed air to ignite a torch.

When the two purveyors of *L'heure bretonne* came to us they were sharply questioned. In Breton. They were asked where they came from. They answered that they didn't speak Breton but that their hearts were very much Breton. Then followed some jostling that caused the wallet of one of the vendors to fall. It contained Belgian identity papers stamped with the swastika. The two men were knocked about and struck. And their newspapers were thrown to the ground during the mêlée. Then suddenly we were in the presence of a feldgendarme that we had not seen arrive. He asked the reason for the fight. While others held back the vendors, two friends and I explained to him in German that it was British propaganda attempting to incite us to rebel against the Marshal and the Germans. As proof we brandished a copy of *L'heure bretonne*. The two men were quiet, protecting their heads with their arms. The feldgendarme took them by the neck.

We had asked the feldgendarme what should be done with the newspapers on the ground and, while rolling one up and putting it in a pocket, we proposed to burn them, which seemed to please him very much. While the German led the two separatists to the police station we lit the papers and swung them like brandons. A little while later we noticed another auto-da-fé elsewhere on the Place where there was a group around Mr. Goaziou, a bookseller known to be close to the bishop.

Instinctively, perhaps intrigued by the sight of seeing the feldgendarmen take the two interlopers to the police station, a crowd followed and found itself grouped together in front of the station. Very quickly individual voices combined to insult the separatists. Then it turned into a tumult, one that pressed against the lower stairs leading to the door. Suddenly the door opened and a German officer came out, camping on the highest step and defying the crowd. After a brief moment of surprise, the insults and complaints began again. The officer then took out a pistol from its case and leveled it at the crowd. He was disconcerted, however, because the crowd guffawed. The officer was hardly impressive with his little revolver, which was better suited to handle a personal duel than to calm a rioting crowd. It was a surreal scene I will never forget. It is true that we were only at the beginning of things, in the summer of 1940.

The door was abruptly opened and the police commissioner appeared. Calling the officer, he had him return inside. Smiling, and addressing himself to the crowd, the commissioner invited it to return home, adding that "that would be best." There was some hesitation, and then someone cried, "To the Kommandantur!" The cry was repeated by several voices. The crowd made a half-turn and descended toward the lower end of the Place, which opens on the Quay of Odet before the prefecture of Finistère, and had been turned into that of the Ortkommandantur. The demonstration at this point had lasted for about an hour. My friends and I arrived on the Quay; the crowd was already there. We found ourselves close to Mr. Goaziou who even though excited by the event kept his cool; while being quite pleased, he was heard to say: "How will all this end?"

There was only one guard in front of the prefecture, which had been closed at the arrival of the crowd. We could see silhouettes apparently observing behind the windows. The crowd and the disturbance grew, but I don't remember any particular chants or slogans. At one point someone intoned "The Marseillaise," but that provoked the anguished response, "Certainly not that!" by the adjutant of the gendarmerie whom we hadn't seen arrive. The crowd picked up again its rumblings.

As noon approached, the rumor ran that German trucks were coming on the nearby roads of Locmaria, returning those on leave who had taken advantage of the Sunday to go bathe at Bénodet. I did not see them, but the crowd began to disperse.

A little after noon, there were only the usual "Sunday strollers," taking a walk before eating. The young Le Bris, my friend Antoine's brother, joined us. We had been told that the Germans had arrested him; he confirmed it. Having made himself conspicuous, he had been arrested after the first part of the demonstration. He had been led to the Kommandantur and retained for more than an hour. An officer had threatened him, waving a revolver under his chin. After the end of the demonstration he had been released, under orders to return to his home not far from there. That was the sole incident of that sort that we noticed at that time.

The next day the press gave an account of that morning. Reading it is very revealing, provided that one knows how to read between the lines after both French and German censorship. One couldn't just ignore the well-known event. During the course of the article the "protest" of "walkers" against the "vendors" became "a scuffle" and the "walkers" were transformed into a "crowd…that destroyed and put to the flame some newspapers." One also read that "all the police forces"—which implied the occupying ones—had "reestablished order" and that there were "arrests" and "inquiries."

The prefect Angéli had the two distributors of *L'heure bretonne* arrested, on the charge that they had disturbed public order. He had actually made use of the occasion because traitors, although condemned by default in May 1940, were protected by the Armistice conventions. Franco-German wrangling occurred, which ended with the sending of the two men to Germany "on probation." Sunday's demonstration was the subject of many commentaries during the course of the week.

Proof that the affair caused a stir: the following Friday the press published a "correction," in order to rectify "different erroneous accounts." The third line [of the correction] reads: "The population of Quimper was indignant, given the current situation, about the attitude of the vendors of the separatist newspaper, that is why the newspapers were ripped from their hands and burned on the spot." The rest of this "subtle propaganda" in the form of an article spoke of the arrests and detention for thirty hours of the two interlopers before being "emancipated by the German authority, who made them immediately leave the town."

The event caused the Vichy representative to intervene with Otto Abetz, but it above all echoed with the German authorities in the region and in Paris. There are numerous reports of this. Finally, on December 12, 1940 there was a directive (n. 1289/40 g. IC office) from the Oberbefelshaber Frankreich General von Stülpnagel on the subject of the "Bretonen frage," the "Breton question."

If this demonstration was not an act of resistance, at least it was a demonstration of the real sentiments of the people of Quimper.

The archives of Finistère and of Majestic have preserved the documents relating to the demonstration.

Soldierly Fraternity or an Act of Resistance in 1940?

Arrested on November 19, 1940 by the police of the Vichy State, who came specially to interrogate us at Sète on the banks of the Marie-Thérèse after we were denounced by some fishermen of the port, my two comrades and I were transferred the next day to the central prison of Montpellier.

About December 2 the commander of the military in the region, General Altmayer, had us brought to his office in order to interrogate us himself. The police had handcuffed us. On my entrance into the office (still accompanied by two inspectors), the general asked me what my service record had been during the Campaign for France. I said that I had received two citations, on the side of Bitche in March, then under Amiens in May-June. Wounded, I had escaped from the Frontlazaret as soon as I was healthy. He asked for a few specifics, including "Who were your leaders?" I told him the truth, that for me they had been magnificent fighters.

After some silence, the general asked me an unexpected question. "How much were you paid?" My reaction was very crude. The general got up, ordered my handcuffs to be removed, and had the police inspectors leave. He told me that unlike my comrades, who had already been demobilized, I had to be brought before the Council of War because the Act of the prefect of Hérault that concerned us specified that we were leaving in order to put ourselves under "the orders of General de Gaulle." It therefore was a "desertion in time of war," because the armistice was not peace. After having left me some time with my morose thoughts General Altmayer then told me that because of my situation as an escapee he instead would apply the directive of Marshal Pétain, higher up as the head of state, who had ordered that escaped prisoners of war be brought to collection camps in the southeast—whence they would be sent to the colonies.

I didn't immediately realize what that would mean for me. My two comrades and I were led back to the prison, but this time not handcuffed, the two policemen escorting us. Two days later my comrades and I left and I received a railroad ticket for Fréjus.

It was not until many years later that I found what could be an explanation for the behavior of the German commandant. It was at the funeral of my former commander of the 2nd Colonial, Captain Darcy. It turns out that the general and my captain were related. That could also explain his questions about my "leaders" in 1940. Did General Altmayer himself perform what resembled an act of resistance as early as 1940?

Final Intervention by Ambassador Albert Chambon

Mr. Chancellor of the Order of the Liberation, Mr. Ambassador, Messrs. Generals, Messrs. Professors, Dear Friends and Comrades.

I don't want to take too much of your time at this point and I am going to try in five or six minutes to convey to you the profound reasons for our gratitude for your presence here. Through everything that you have had the opportunity to say, you, our American friends, you, the professors, and you, the witnesses, you have taught us many things.

Why are we so grateful to you? Because you answer exactly to the three goals that the Club Témoin, from its beginning, has proposed to itself.

The first of these goals: To try to end the tall tales that have proliferated—since the Liberation—about the Occupation, the Resistance, the deportation, and God knows what else. Some are so ridiculous one doesn't dare repeat them. These tall tales bothered us resisters even at the time. A long time ago we left the Resistance and we have assumed our official responsibilities. Personally, I was a diplomat. But fifty years after, to see these tall tales persist, that bothers us. What will our children, our grandchildren, the future generations, think? That is why we have created the Club Témoin. That is why.

The most extraordinary tall tale belongs to the party that claims to be the party of "the shot dead," because—they say—there were 75,000 shot dead among them. There were 12,400 shot dead for all of France from all political opinions, of all ages, from all social conditions!

Three years ago at the time of the presidential elections I heard a candidate of that same party being interviewed on television, and he spoke of the 75,000 shot dead. Fifty years later, no, that cannot stand.

Albert Chambon is the founder and president of the Club Témoin.

161

And no one on the television show, no one of the people who inter-viewed him, no one dared to say to him, "but Mr. President or candi-date for the presidency, really, that's astonishing, because there weren't even 75,000 French in total shot dead." This is one of the principal reasons why we created this association.

We have thought of those who have been the most forgotten, be-side the 100,000 comrades fallen on the field of battle and honor in June 1940, all those people that you have spoken about with elo-quence and exactness, that unrecognized resistance. You have spo-ken about all these comrades who helped the escapees, those who were being hunted....

But the unrecognized resistance extended to everyone. Person-ally, I am a former official. How many officials were in the Resis-tance in 1941-1942? More than 100,000. Where were they? In the NAP (the Infiltration of Public Administration), in the super-NAP (the Infiltration of the High Administrations). I speak of what I know, as I represented Foreign Affairs in the super-NAP. We therefore—the 100,000 members of this NAP—were officials.

But how many unpaid people were there? Me, I had at least six or seven. Therefore, when one speaks of 300,000 or 400,000 resisters, one is very mistaken, one leaves out and denigrates many. One deni-grates all those people who have disappeared, all these comrades. I could never find them; they didn't know who I was and I didn't know who they were.

There were 400,000 cardholders who were resisters, but one must multiply that figure by five or six if you want to know the truth. Weygand was right: there are close to three million French who all participated in the Resistance. Why then these tall tales?

One must not get upset, though. Why should one not be too sur-prised? Because, for four years the Resistance had a gag in its mouth. No one spoke about us; we couldn't speak about ourselves. The condition of safety was to say nothing and not to cause talk about ourselves. As my friend, Susie Bidault, the wife of the former presi-dent of the CNR, said: we were "like moles" and, she added, "we have remained moles."

That's why it really is very difficult, why it is almost impossible to write a history of the Resistance. Why can't one write the history of the Resistance? Because during four years we were in total silence, but above all because in the Resistance everything was very compartmentalized, very partitioned. It was a question of safety, even in the same movement. Me, at a certain point I had an office beside the Saint-Lazare station and my network head was in the 16th arrondissement beside Place Victor Hugo. We saw each other once every two months. It was a matter of safety not to see each other. One therefore can write a history of our resistance but not the history of the Resistance. No.

That is one of the first reasons. The second reason is that there weren't any archives of the Resistance. To write a word was dangerous; one risked being arrested. One must never write anything. Therefore there aren't any archives.

Finally, reflect a moment. All these people, like everyone, were in danger. They didn't write the truth; they wrote what they thought they must write to the person to whom they wrote. All the archives of those days are falsified. In fact, I'm inclined to believe that the declarations of the German generals who were in France and conducted reprisals were sometimes the most credible accounts we have.

The "unrecognized resistance" has been ignored since the Liberation. No one, except for the Club Témoin, has organized a public gathering to put an end to this silence concerning all the "little people" who labored as we did, who merit as much as we do a decoration, and who have never received public recognition—until now.

The history of the Resistance was never written. Perhaps I exaggerate. Yes, there was one that was written; it was by Henri Frenay.

De Gaulle was in London. In France, in the Resistance, on our native soil, it was Henri Frenay who was our head. If anyone wants to know what the Resistance truly was, there is only one book to read, one book, *La nuit finira* (*The Night will End*) by Henri Frenay. Yes, Frenay has admirably written the history of the Resistance, and very succinctly too, since he went to the essentials. But of course, happily, there are many historians who have written admirable books about all the details: the underground, the operations in Brittany with 35,000 members of the underground, the parachute drops, and all sorts of things like that.

To be sure, all of that is the history of the Resistance, but what is behind that history? Ask that question and Frenay will say to you: "If you only think of all these facts you know nothing about the Resistance, nothing, because the Resistance was a flame, a torch, a breath that animated us and that desired not only that we boot the

Germans out of France but also that we would try to build a more just, more fraternal, more humane world than the one we knew."

Because we were the children of the heroes of the War of 1914-1918, we knew that this already was the dream of our parents. For us though it was at least as much. I was going to say, even more so. Why? Remember history.

When we left we didn't leave singing, as we did in 1914. We left with the idea that when we will have ousted the Germans from France, we will do everything to create a more just, more fraternal, more humane world. And that we have done.

When you read Frenay, you will understand that truly we have done so. If that goal revealed itself not to be totally feasible, that isn't our fault.... Frenay too let that be known. And I myself have written a book to say why. But it was the breath, the flame that animated us. It was—beyond fighting against the Germans—to create a more just, fraternal, and humane world.

That is why today you have contributed to, even expanded, our second mission or goal. We want to transmit to our children and our grandchildren this flame of the Resistance. "Resistance" is not the fact of a period—in life "resistance" is a daily matter. Today France is in as much danger, I myself would say more danger, than in 1940. Resistance is just as necessary.

What, then, is resistance? Resistance is to risk your own life in order to say no, when the interests, the sovereignty, the independence, the liberty of France are at stake.

In this association that we have created, from the beginning we wanted one-half resisters, one-half people of the generation after the war. Today those who lead the Club are all people born after the Liberation and our treasurer, I believe, is barely twenty-nine or thirty years old. I would like to compliment all the members of the Club Témoin, our comrades, born after the Liberation. It is thanks to them that this colloquium was as successful as it has been. It is thanks to them.

And then our third goal. It pertains to you, too. It is to remain faithful to our allies, to all our allies. To be sure, after the Liberation it was necessary to reconcile with Germany. There could be no peace in Europe without reconciliation with Germany, that goes without saying. This reconciliation—sincere and complete—has occurred.

Does that mean that we have forgotten? Certainly not. No, we haven't forgotten. We have seen children at Bréhal, sixty innocent children, who were suspended from balconies by General Lammerding, who was furious that he couldn't get to the beaches at Normandy quicker. A little further, 540 women and children were burned alive in a church where I went to Mass when I was a child in Limousin.[1] No, we haven't forgotten. But we have forgiven. Forgiven from our heart because France is a fundamentally Christian nation. The great German-born philosopher Hannah Arendt was right when she spoke of the power of the virtue of forgiveness.

And if we haven't forgotten these terrible times, we have even less forgotten everything that our allies brought and did, all our allies.

Today I praise and thank the glorious British people. Churchill was right to say that, perhaps, never in the history of humanity have so few people saved the lives of so many. That is true.

And we haven't forgotten the sacrifices of the Russian troops who defeated the fanatical Wehrmarcht that we first fought on the plains of France in June 1940. We haven't forgotten that it was at Stalingrad that the fanatical Wehrmarcht was defeated.

Nor have we forgotten our American allies. How can you expect us not to be filled with extraordinary emotion!... To see General Vernon Walters, the glorious combatant on the fields of battle in Europe, Africa, and Asia and who believed himself duty-bound to take the trouble to come today and speak to us. We are immensely grateful to him.

How can you expect us not to have immense gratitude toward President Patton, representing all the glorious parachutists and pilots who fell on the field of battle, the field of honor? Everywhere, they died extraordinarily, heroically. And you know that it wasn't by the thousands, but by the tens of thousands.

Mr. Patton, I would be obliged to you if you would say to all your comrades that not only have we not forgotten but that nothing will ever break the friendship between our two countries, or our gratitude, because it was sealed in blood by thousands of your heroic pilots. Please tell them that in politics between nations—this must be—there will be disagreements from time to time. But the French people and all of France remain totally attached to you with our deepest gratitude and friendship. Long live the United States, long live France.

Note

1.   Oradour-sur-Glane (Haute-Vienne).

General Conclusions by the General of the Army (CR) Jean Simon, Chancellor of the Order of the Liberation

After all that has been well and truly said, it seems to me rather difficult to draw the conclusions from this entire colloquium and to put into relief all the unrecognized resistances.

Nonetheless, I would like to reiterate that the French people as a whole were much more "resistant" and combative than is sometimes said.

Moreover, when we fought (I speak of the Free French to which I belonged) in Abyssinia, in Eritria, in Libya, in Tripoli, and elsewhere, our fight would have had no meaning if we hadn't known that in France men and women were resisting. That braced us, gave us the necessary energy. If there hadn't been those fighters in France, we would have simply been mercenaries and our fight would absolutely not have had the same significance.

I also want to say that under General de Gaulle's direction we always received extraordinarily precise orders. General de Gaulle never abandoned us, never, even in the worst moments; I allude to the setbacks we had, especially at Dakar.

We left for Dakar thinking that we were going to be received with laurels and triumphs. We were welcomed with cannons. I am not here to redo history...that is a fact. Obviously, morale was very low. But nonetheless there was the following: after the expedition we regrouped at Freetown and General de Gaulle assembled all his officers; no one reproved the General and we continued to act and to fight, fortified by the thought that our comrades in the Resistance were fighting. That encouraged us when there were lapses in our morale.

I have to say that General de Gaulle was a rather astonishing man when one worked close to him, which often happened to me. He

167

was a man who, one might say, gave orders to history. After the
setback of Dakar he told us, "Well, that is a painful blow," but then
he sketched everything that we would do in the following three years,
which was exactly what we ended up doing. He told us, "We are
going to divide into two groups; one group will go by the Mediterranean coast lines, the other by the Middle East" (which is what I did).

But what is even more extraordinary is that he told us the date. He
said, "These two groups will meet up in February 1943 on the banks
of the Mediterranean." Which is what happened. Thus we had complete confidence in him.

And, as I said, your activity comforted us. And that, very simply,
is what I wanted to tell you. Thank you for having participated in a
colloquium of such a high quality.

Name Index